Table of Contents

Conquer
Your Mindset

ReDefine
Your Success

...BOOK 2

Sajjad Mundia

Conquer Your Mindset
ReDefine Your Success
Book 2

By

Sajjad Mundia

Copyright

Disclaimer

The information provided in this book is for general informational purposes only. The author is not a licensed therapist, psychologist, or medical professional. The content within this book is based on personal experiences, research, and observations.

The practices, techniques, and advice presented in this book are intended to provide guidance and tools for self-awareness, personal growth, and emotional well-being. However, they should not be considered a substitute for professional advice, diagnosis, or treatment. Readers are encouraged to seek advice from qualified professionals regarding specific questions or concerns about their mental health or well-being.

The author and publisher of this book make no representations or warranties of any kind, express or implied, about the completeness, accuracy, reliability, suitability, or availability of the information contained within these pages. Any reliance you place on such information is therefore strictly at your own risk.

The author and publisher disclaim any liability for any loss, damage, or injury caused by the use or misuse of the information provided in this book. The reader assumes full responsibility for their actions and decisions based on the content of this book.

All product names, logos, and brands mentioned within this book are the property of their respective owners and are used for identification purposes only. Their inclusion does not imply any endorsement or affiliation with the book.

By reading this book, you agree to these terms and acknowledge that the author and publisher are not responsible for any consequences resulting from the use of the information provided herein.

Table of Contents

Chapter 6: Cultivating Positive Habits

Chapter 7: Gratitude and Positive Affirmations

- Discuss the science behind gratitude and brain function.
- Introduce the concept of a gratitude journal.
- Creating a Positive Affirmation Practice
- Discuss the role of affirmations in mindset transformation.
- Provide guidelines for crafting powerful affirmations.
- Introduce the use of affirmations in visualization.
- Expressing Gratitude in Relationships
- Explore the impact of gratitude on interpersonal relationships.
- Discuss the role of appreciation in fostering connection.
- Provide actionable steps for expressing gratitude.
- Overcoming Negativity Bias with Positivity
- Discuss the negativity bias and its impact on mindset.
- Provide strategies for overcoming negativity bias.
- Explore the role of positive affirmations in challenging negative thoughts.
- Gratitude as a Lifestyle
- Discuss the transition from occasional practice to a lifestyle of gratitude.
- Share stories of individuals transformed by a gratitude mindset.
- Provide practical tips for maintaining a grateful perspective.

Chapter 8: Mindful Decision Making

- "Your life is a result of the decisions you make. Explore the art of mindful decision-making for a purposeful mindset."
- Understanding Decision-Making Processes
- Discuss the cognitive processes involved in decision-making.
- Explore the impact of emotions on choices.
- Introduce the concept of decision fatigue.
- Mindful Decision-Making Techniques
- Introduce mindfulness techniques for decision-making.
- Discuss the importance of clarity in decision-making.
- Provide a step-by-step guide to mindful decision-making.
- Overcoming Decision Paralysis
- Discuss common challenges leading to decision paralysis.
- Provide strategies for overcoming indecision.

- Explore the role of mindset in breaking decision-making patterns.
- Aligning Decisions with Values and Goals
- Explore the importance of aligning decisions with personal values.
- Discuss the role of goals in guiding decision-making.
- Provide exercises for clarifying values and setting decision criteria.
- Learning from Decisions, Whether Positive or Negative
- Discuss the value of learning from both successful and failed decisions.
- Explore the mindset of continuous improvement.
- Provide reflective exercises to extract lessons from past decisions.

Chapter 9: Nurturing Positive Relationships

- "The company you keep influences your mindset. Explore the transformative impact of positive relationships on mindset mastery."
- Understanding the Relationship-Mindset Connection
- Explore the reciprocal influence of relationships and mindset.
- Discuss the impact of social support on personal growth.
- Introduce the concept of toxic relationships.
- Cultivating Positive Connections
- Provide actionable steps for building positive relationships.
- Discuss the importance of empathy in connections.
- Explore the role of effective communication in fostering positive relationships.
- Setting Healthy Boundaries
- Discuss the importance of boundaries in relationships.
- Provide guidance on setting and communicating boundaries.
- Explore the impact of boundary-setting on mindset.
- Navigating Conflict with a Growth Mindset
- Discuss common sources of conflict in relationships.
- Explore conflict resolution strategies.
- Introduce the concept of using challenges to strengthen relationships.
- Fostering a Supportive Network for Mindset Mastery
- Emphasize the role of a supportive network in mindset transformation.
- Discuss the impact of peer influence on mindset.
- Provide guidance on cultivating a positive social environment.

Chapter 10: Sustainable Mindset Mastery

- "Mindset mastery is a lifelong journey. Discover the keys to sustaining a positive and growth-oriented mindset for lasting success."
  - Reflecting on the Journey
  - Encourage readers to reflect on their mindset transformation.
  - Provide prompts for self-assessment.
  - Celebrate the progress made in the mindset mastery journey.
  - Creating a Personalized Mindset Maintenance Plan
  - Guide readers in developing a sustainable mindset maintenance plan.
  - Discuss the role of ongoing learning and growth.
  - Provide tools for adapting the plan to evolving life circumstances.
  - Mindset Mastery Beyond the Individual
  - Explore the broader impact of mindset mastery on communities and organizations.
  - Discuss the role of mindset in societal progress.
  - Encourage readers to share and spread the mindset mastery journey.
  - Staying Connected to Growth
  - Provide strategies for staying connected to personal growth.
  - Discuss the importance of regular mindset check-ins.
  - Explore the concept of mentorship in sustaining mindset mastery.
  - Empowering Others to Master Their Mindset
  - Share stories of individuals who inspired others through mindset mastery.
  - Discuss the ripple effect of a positive mindset on those around us.
  - Encourage readers to become ambassadors of mindset mastery.

Conclusion

- Summary of Key Takeaways
  - Recap the essential concepts explored in each chapter.
  - Emphasize the transformative power of mindset mastery.
  - Final Words of Encouragement
  - Motivate readers to continue their mindset mastery journey.
  - Provide a final inspirational quote or anecdote.

- Call to Action
- Encourage readers to apply the principles learned in the book.
- Provide resources for ongoing support and learning.

Chapter 6
Cultivating Positive Habits

Understanding the Habit Loop

Did you know that on average, about 40% of our daily actions are not decisions, but habits? Imagine if you could unravel the mystery behind these habits and use them to your advantage in mastering your mindset. Well, that's exactly what we're about to dive into.

Habits are like invisible threads woven into the fabric of our daily lives. Understanding the Habit Loop is like discovering the secret code to these threads, allowing you to reshape them in ways that empower your mindset.

Breaking Down the Habit Loop

Cue: The Trigger

- The habit loop kicks off with a cue, a trigger that sets everything in motion.
- Cues can be anything from a specific time of day to an emotional state or a particular location.
- Example: Feeling stressed (cue) prompts you to bite your nails (habit).

Routine: The Behavior

- This is the actual behavior or action triggered by the cue.
- Habits are often automatic responses, requiring minimal conscious thought.
- Example: Nail-biting in response to stress becomes the routine.

Reward: The Reinforcement

- The routine leads to a reward, a positive outcome that reinforces the habit loop.
- Rewards can be physical, emotional, or psychological.
- Example: Nail-biting might provide a momentary sense of relief from stress (reward).

The Power of Awareness

Recognizing the habit loop is the first step towards mastering it. By identifying cues, routines, and rewards, you gain control over your behaviors, allowing you to replace detrimental habits with positive ones that contribute to your mindset mastery.

Explore the Habit Loop: Cue, Routine, Reward

Ever wondered why some habits are so hard to break, while others seem to effortlessly stick? The answer lies in the intricate dance between the cue, routine, and reward. Let's unravel this dance and discover how it shapes our everyday lives.

The Cue: Unmasking Triggers

- Cues can be categorized into different types: time-based, emotion-based, location-based, and social-based.
- Identifying your cues requires a bit of self-reflection. Keep a habit journal to note down what triggers your routines.
- Example: If you habitually snack at a certain time, the time itself acts as the cue.

The Routine: Unveiling Actions

- Routines are the visible part of habits, the actions we take.
- Breaking down routines into smaller, manageable steps makes it easier to replace them with positive behaviors.
- Example: If you snack when bored, replace it with a short walk or a quick mindfulness exercise.

The Reward: Unearthing Pleasures

- Rewards can be tricky to pinpoint but are essential for habit formation.
- Experiment with different rewards to find healthier alternatives that satisfy the underlying need.
- Example: Instead of the fleeting pleasure of a sugary snack, savor the satisfaction of completing a task.

Rewiring the Loop

● Once you understand the cue, routine, and reward, experiment with adjusting one element at a time.

    ● Gradual changes make habit transformation more sustainable.

    ● Example: Shift the routine of snacking to a healthier option, like a piece of fruit or a handful of nuts.

Discuss How Habits Shape Mindset

Your habits are not just idle actions; they are the architects shaping the very foundation of your mindset. Let's explore how these seemingly small routines have a profound impact on the way you perceive the world and yourself.

The Subtle Influence of Habits

● Habits influence your thoughts and beliefs by reinforcing certain patterns of behavior.

    ● Negative habits can create a fixed mindset, while positive habits contribute to a growth mindset.

    ● Example: Consistently practicing gratitude can shift your mindset from scarcity to abundance.

The Feedback Loop

● Habits create a feedback loop, influencing not only your actions but also your self-perception.

    ● Positive habits enhance self-esteem, while negative habits may erode it.

    ● Example: Regular exercise not only improves physical health but also boosts confidence and self-worth.

Shaping Perspectives

● Habits shape the lens through which you view challenges and opportunities.

    ● A habitually positive outlook can lead to resilience and adaptability.

    ● Example: Facing setbacks with a growth mindset allows you to see them as opportunities for learning and improvement.

Introduce the Concept of Keystone Habits

Imagine having a magical key that, when turned, unlocks a cascade of positive changes in your life. Welcome to the realm of keystone habits, where small shifts lead to significant transformations.

The Keystone Concept

- Keystone habits are small, manageable changes that have a disproportionate impact on other areas of your life.
  - These habits act as catalysts, triggering a domino effect of positive behaviors.
  - Example: Regular exercise often leads to improved sleep, better nutrition, and increased productivity.

Identifying Keystone Habits

- Look for habits that naturally lead to other positive behaviors.
  - Keystone habits often align with your core values and long-term goals.
  - Example: If your goal is to enhance focus and productivity, a keystone habit might be establishing a daily meditation practice.

Building a Keystone Habit

- Start small and focus on consistency.
  - Celebrate small victories to reinforce the habit loop.
  - Example: Begin with a five-minute meditation each morning and gradually extend the duration as it becomes a natural part of your routine.

Closing Thoughts

Understanding the intricacies of the habit loop, exploring its components, recognizing the influence on mindset, and embracing keystone habits are crucial steps on your journey to mindset mastery. By unraveling the threads of your habits, you gain the power to weave a tapestry of positive change, unlocking your full potential.

Identifying and Breaking Negative Habits

"Breaking free from negative habits is like shedding the weight of self-doubt and stepping into the light of empowerment. Let's embark on a journey to identify and dismantle these habits, unlocking the door to your full potential."

Understanding Negative Habits

Recognizing the Red Flags

- Negative habits often manifest as repetitive, unproductive behaviors that hinder personal growth.

- Pay attention to feelings of guilt, frustration, or stagnation – these may indicate harmful habits.

- Example: Procrastination leading to missed deadlines could be a sign of a negative habit.

Exploring the Impact

- Negative habits can have a domino effect, affecting various aspects of your life.

- Analyze how these habits contribute to stress, hinder relationships, or impede professional success.

- Example: Excessive screen time might be impacting your sleep quality, energy levels, and overall well-being.

Guide Readers in Identifying Detrimental Habits

"Imagine having a personal detective kit to unveil the hidden culprits sabotaging your progress. Let's equip you with the tools to identify detrimental habits and take back control of your life."

Self-Reflection and Observation

Keep a Habit Journal
- Document your daily routines and behaviors.
- Note down situations triggering certain habits and your emotional state during those moments.
- Example: Recording instances of stress leading to emotional eating.

Solicit Feedback
- Seek input from friends, family, or colleagues about habits they observe in you.
- External perspectives can offer valuable insights into blind spots.
- Example: Friends may point out patterns of negativity or self-sabotage in your language.

Triggers and Patterns

Identify Triggers
- Pinpoint the cues that initiate negative habits.
- Triggers can be emotional, environmental, or situational.
- Example: Feeling lonely as a trigger for excessive social media scrolling.

Recognize Patterns
- Notice recurring themes or routines associated with detrimental habits.
- Understanding patterns makes it easier to interrupt and replace them.
- Example: Consistently hitting the snooze button leading to rushed mornings.

Discuss the Psychology of Habit Formation

"Unraveling the mysteries of habit formation is like decoding your own behavior. Let's delve into the fascinating psychology behind habits, unveiling the forces that shape our actions and mindset."

The Habit Loop Revisited

Cue, Routine, Reward

- Reiterating the three components of the habit loop.
- Understanding how cues trigger routines and lead to rewards.
- Example: The cue of boredom (Cue) leading to online shopping (Routine) and the reward of temporary pleasure (Reward).

Neuroplasticity and Habit Pathways

Neuroplasticity

- The brain's ability to rewire itself.
- Habits create neural pathways that strengthen with repetition.
- Example: Regular exercise forming new neural connections related to motivation and well-being.

Dopamine and Rewards

- Dopamine, the brain's reward neurotransmitter.
- Habits release dopamine, reinforcing the behavior.
- Example: Checking social media generating a dopamine hit, reinforcing the habit of constant scrolling.

The Role of Beliefs

Core Beliefs

- Habits are often rooted in underlying beliefs about oneself.
- Negative beliefs can fuel detrimental habits.
- Example: Low self-esteem leading to the habit of seeking constant validation.

Provide Strategies for Breaking Negative Habits

"Imagine having a toolbox filled with strategies to dismantle the walls of negative habits. Let's equip you with effective techniques to break free and pave the way for positive change."

Gradual Replacement

Introduce Positive Alternatives
- Identify a positive behavior to replace the negative habit.
- Gradually integrate the new behavior into the existing routine.
- Example: Replace mindless snacking with a five-minute stretching routine.

Mindfulness and Awareness

Practice Mindful Awareness
- Cultivate awareness of triggers and cues.
- Mindfulness helps interrupt automatic responses.
- Example: When feeling stressed, pause, take a deep breath, and assess whether you truly need to engage in the negative habit.

Mindful Eating
- Apply mindfulness to eating habits, paying attention to hunger and satiety cues.
- Avoid emotional eating by staying present during meals.
- Example: Savoring each bite and recognizing when you are satisfied.

Accountability and Support

Share Goals with Others
- Inform friends or family about your intention to break a habit.
- Accountability fosters commitment.
- Example: Having a workout buddy to encourage regular exercise.

Seek Professional Support
- Consult with a therapist or coach for guidance.
- Professionals provide personalized strategies and emotional support.

- Example: Working with a therapist to address the root causes of a detrimental habit.

Celebrate Progress

Acknowledge Small Wins

- Celebrate each step towards breaking a negative habit.
- Positive reinforcement enhances motivation.
- Example: Acknowledge a week of reduced screen time as a significant achievement.

In the quest for mindset mastery, identifying and breaking negative habits is a pivotal step. Armed with self-awareness and effective strategies, you can dismantle the barriers holding you back, paving the way for a positive and empowered mindset.

Establishing Positive Rituals

"Imagine having a magic wand that could transform your day. Well, positive rituals are that magic wand, and we're about to uncover the secrets of weaving them into your life, unlocking the gateway to your full potential."

Understanding Positive Rituals

Defining Positive Rituals

- Positive rituals are intentional, repeated behaviors designed to enhance well-being and mindset.
- Unlike habits, rituals carry a sense of meaning and purpose.
- Example: Daily gratitude journaling as a positive ritual to foster a positive mindset.

The Power of Intent

- Intent distinguishes rituals from routine actions.
- Each ritual should be a conscious choice aligning with your values and goals.
- Example: Setting an intention before meditation, focusing on mindfulness and self-reflection.

Discuss the Power of Positive Daily Rituals

"Daily rituals are the quiet architects shaping the grand design of your life. Let's dive into the immense power these seemingly small actions hold and how they can fuel your journey towards mindset mastery."

Impact on Mindset

Setting the Tone for the Day

• Morning rituals establish a positive tone, influencing the mindset for the entire day.

• Positive mornings often lead to increased resilience and productivity.

• Example: Starting the day with a few minutes of gratitude can shift your mindset towards positivity.

Creating Moments of Reflection

• Evening rituals provide a space for reflection and closure.

• Reflection helps process the day, fostering gratitude and self-awareness.

• Example: Journaling before bed to reflect on achievements and lessons learned.

Enhancing Emotional Well-being

Stress Reduction

• Positive rituals act as buffers against stress.

• Engaging in activities you enjoy can alleviate stress and contribute to emotional resilience.

• Example: Taking a short nature walk during lunch as a stress-relieving ritual.

Boosting Positive Emotions

• Daily rituals contribute to a steady influx of positive emotions.

• Consistent positive experiences foster an overall positive emotional state.

• Example: Ending the day with a brief meditation to cultivate feelings of peace and contentment.

Provide Examples of Impactful Morning and

Evening Routines

"Ever wondered what makes successful individuals tick in the morning and wind down in the evening? Let's peek into the daily rituals of high achievers, exploring the habits that set the stage for their success."

Impactful Morning Routines

Early Wake-up with Purpose
- Early risers often attribute their success to a purposeful start.
- Use the quiet morning hours for personal development or strategic planning.
- Example: Waking up 30 minutes earlier for meditation or goal-setting.

Mindful Movement
- Incorporating exercise into the morning routine enhances physical and mental well-being.
- Movement releases endorphins, boosting mood and energy levels.
- Example: A quick home workout or a brisk walk to kickstart the day.

Nourishing Breakfast
- A nutritious breakfast provides essential fuel for the day.
- Eating mindfully fosters a positive relationship with food.
- Example: A balanced breakfast with whole grains, fruits, and protein.

Impactful Evening Routines

Digital Detox
- Disconnecting from screens before bedtime improves sleep quality.
- Create a relaxing bedtime routine to signal the body that it's time to wind down.
- Example: Dimming lights and avoiding screens for at least an hour before sleep.

Gratitude Journaling
- Reflecting on positive aspects of the day cultivates gratitude.
- Gratitude journaling contributes to a positive mindset.
- Example: Listing three things you're grateful for before going to bed.

Mindful Relaxation

- Engaging in calming activities prepares the mind for restful sleep.
- Activities like reading or gentle stretching signal relaxation.
- Example: Reading a book or practicing deep breathing exercises.

Explore the Role of Consistency in Habit Formation

"Consistency is the secret sauce that turns rituals into powerful habits. Let's unravel the science behind the magic of doing things repeatedly, day in and day out, and how it shapes your mindset over time."

The Science of Consistency

Neurological Impact

- Consistent actions create and strengthen neural pathways in the brain.
- Habits become more automatic with repetition.
- Example: Regular mindfulness practice rewires the brain for increased focus and emotional regulation.

Behavioral Patterns

- Consistency forms behavioral patterns that become ingrained over time.
- Repeated positive rituals contribute to the formation of positive habits.
- Example: Daily exercise becoming a natural and enjoyable part of your routine.

Overcoming Challenges

Start Small, Stay Steady

- Begin with manageable rituals to build consistency.
- Gradually increase complexity or duration as the behavior becomes ingrained.
- Example: Starting with a five-minute meditation and extending it gradually.

Accountability Systems

- Share your rituals with a friend or family member to create external accountability.
- Having a supportive community can make consistency more achievable.
- Example: Finding a workout partner to encourage regular exercise.

Closing Thoughts

Positive rituals, when woven into your daily life with intent and consistency, have the power to shape your mindset and propel you towards your full potential. As you embark on this journey, remember that small, intentional actions, repeated consistently, can lead to profound transformations in your life.

Mindful Habits for Well-Being

"Imagine weaving a tapestry of well-being into the fabric of your life. Mindful habits are the gentle strokes that create this masterpiece, and we're about to explore the intricacies of cultivating a mindful existence for your overall well-being."

Understanding Mindful Habits

What are Mindful Habits?

- Mindful habits involve engaging in daily activities with full awareness and intention.
- These habits contribute to a state of mindfulness, fostering a deeper connection with the present moment.
- Example: Mindfully savoring a cup of tea, paying attention to each sip and the warmth it brings.

The Impact on Well-being

- Mindful habits enhance emotional resilience and mental clarity.
- Regular practice contributes to reduced stress, improved focus, and increased overall happiness.
- Example: Taking a few mindful breaths during a hectic day to reset and refocus.

Introduce Mindfulness as a Habit

"Ever wished for a reset button in the chaos of life? Well, mindfulness is the ultimate reset, and we're about to introduce it not as a distant goal but as a simple and accessible habit that can transform your daily experience."

Demystifying Mindfulness

Beyond Meditation

- Mindfulness is not limited to formal meditation.
- It's a state of open awareness that can be integrated into everyday activities.
- Example: Mindfully washing dishes, feeling the water, and being present with each movement.

Accessible to All

- Mindfulness is a practice available to everyone, regardless of age or background.
- It doesn't require special skills; it's about cultivating a mindful attitude.
- Example: Children can practice mindfulness by paying full attention while playing or eating.

The Mindful Pause

Bringing Attention to the Breath

- The breath serves as an anchor to the present moment.
- Taking a mindful pause to focus on the breath helps center the mind.
- Example: Inhaling deeply, feeling the breath fill the lungs, and exhaling slowly.

Integration into Daily Routine

- Introduce short mindful pauses throughout the day.
- These moments can be integrated into routine activities like commuting, working, or waiting in line.
- Example: Taking a mindful pause before responding to an email or during a short break at work.

Discuss Mindful Eating, Breathing, and Presence

"What if the simple act of eating, breathing, and being present could become sources of profound well-being? Let's delve into the transformative power of mindful habits in these fundamental aspects of life."

Mindful Eating

Savoring Each Bite

- Mindful eating involves paying full attention to the sensory experience of eating.
- It promotes gratitude for the nourishment provided by food.
- Example: Noticing the texture, taste, and aroma of each bite during a meal.

Listening to Hunger and Fullness Cues

- Mindful eating encourages tuning into internal cues of hunger and fullness.
- This practice fosters a healthier relationship with food.
- Example: Eating when hungry and stopping when satisfied, rather than following external cues.

Mindful Breathing

The Breath as an Anchor

- Mindful breathing involves bringing awareness to the natural rhythm of the breath.
- It serves as a grounding anchor during moments of stress or distraction.
- Example: Taking a few conscious breaths when feeling overwhelmed.

Body Scan for Relaxation

- Mindful breathing can be extended into a body scan, bringing awareness to each part of the body.
- This practice promotes relaxation and release of tension.
- Example: Inhaling and exhaling while mentally scanning from head to toe, releasing tension with each breath.

Mindful Presence

Being Present in Daily Activities

- Mindfulness extends to being fully present in routine activities.

- It involves letting go of distractions and immersing oneself in the current task.

- Example: Being fully present while taking a walk, noticing the surroundings, and feeling each step.

Mindful Listening

- Mindful presence includes active and attentive listening.

- It fosters deeper connections in relationships and reduces misunderstandings.

- Example: Listening without formulating a response, fully absorbing the speaker's words.

Provide Practical Exercises for Incorporating Mindfulness into Daily Life

"Let's turn theory into practice. These simple yet impactful exercises will seamlessly integrate mindfulness into your daily routine, paving the way for a more mindful and fulfilling life."

Mindful Breathing Exercise

Box Breathing

- Inhale for a count of four, hold the breath for four counts, exhale for four counts, and then pause for another four counts.
- Repeat for several cycles.
- Example: Practice box breathing during a short break or before a challenging task.

Mindful Eating Exercise

The Five Senses Meal

- Engage all five senses while eating a meal.
- Notice the colors, textures, smells, sounds, and flavors.
- Example: Try the five senses meal with a simple dish, paying attention to each sensory aspect.

Mindful Presence Exercise

One-Minute Mindfulness

- Set aside one minute to focus completely on your breath or a chosen object.
- Let go of distractions and bring your attention back whenever the mind wanders.
- Example: Use the one-minute mindfulness exercise during moments of stress or when transitioning between tasks.

Closing Thoughts

Cultivating mindful habits for well-being is a journey of simplicity and profound impact. As you embark on this path, remember that mindfulness is not about perfection but about the intention to be present in each moment. By incorporating these mindful habits into your life, you are unlocking the door to a more peaceful, purposeful, and fulfilling existence.

Sustaining Positive Habits for Long-Term Success

"Imagine positive habits as seeds you plant, and with consistent care, they grow into mighty trees of success. Let's delve into the secrets of sustaining these habits, ensuring your journey towards mindset mastery is not just a sprint but a lifelong marathon."

The Power of Consistency

Consistency as the Cornerstone

- Long-term success is rooted in the soil of consistency.
- Consistent positive habits create a foundation for lasting change.
- Example: Daily mindfulness practice gradually reshaping the neural pathways in the brain.

The Compound Effect

- Small positive actions, when repeated consistently, yield significant results over time.
- The compound effect is the magic of consistent effort accumulating into transformative outcomes.
- Example: Saving a small amount regularly leads to substantial wealth over the years.

Discuss the Challenges of Maintaining Positive Habits

"The path to positive habits isn't always a smooth walk; there are bumps, detours, and the occasional stumble. Let's navigate through the common challenges, ensuring you're well-prepared for the twists on your journey towards lasting positive change."

Common Challenges

Initial Enthusiasm vs. Long-Term Commitment

- Many struggle with maintaining positive habits beyond the initial burst of enthusiasm.
- Long-term commitment requires a shift from excitement to a deeper understanding of the habit's value.
- Example: Starting a fitness routine with gusto but finding it challenging to stick with it over time.

Overcoming Plateaus

- Progress often plateaus, and habits may lose their initial novelty.
- Plateaus can lead to frustration and a decline in motivation.
- Example: Learning a new skill initially feels exciting, but the plateau phase might make it seem less rewarding.

Provide Strategies for Overcoming Obstacles

"In the face of challenges, resilience becomes your greatest ally. Let's arm you with effective strategies to navigate the hurdles, ensuring you not only start strong but also finish even stronger in your pursuit of positive habits."

Practical Strategies

Set Realistic Expectations
- Acknowledge that challenges are part of the journey.
- Set realistic expectations to avoid feeling overwhelmed.
- Example: Understanding that occasional setbacks are normal and part of the learning process.

Celebrate Small Wins
- Acknowledge and celebrate each small achievement.
- Recognizing progress boosts motivation and reinforces positive habits.
- Example: Celebrating a week of consistent exercise or a month of mindful eating.

Adapt and Adjust
- Be willing to adapt your approach based on changing circumstances.
- Flexibility allows for the sustainability of positive habits.
- Example: Adjusting your workout routine to accommodate a busy schedule.

Establish Support Systems
- Share your goals with friends, family, or a supportive community.
- Having a support system provides encouragement during challenging times.
- Example: Joining a fitness class or having a workout buddy for mutual motivation.

Emphasize the Cumulative Impact of Sustained Positive Habits on Mindset Mastery

"Picture sustained positive habits as the steady rain that nurtures the seeds of your mindset, allowing them to bloom into a garden of empowerment. Let's explore the profound impact of consistent positive actions on your journey towards mindset mastery."

The Ripple Effect

Positive Habits as Mindset Shapers
- Sustained positive habits contribute to the formation of a growth mindset.
- Consistent effort fosters a belief in continuous improvement and resilience.
- Example: Regular learning and skill development reinforcing the belief that growth is possible.

Building Confidence
- Accomplishing positive habits over time boosts self-confidence.
- Confidence becomes a catalyst for taking on more significant challenges.
- Example: Successfully completing a daily writing habit leading to the confidence to tackle larger writing projects.

The Transformational Journey

Mindset as a Dynamic Process
- Mindset mastery is not a destination but a continuous journey.
- Consistent positive habits create a mindset that embraces change and continuous improvement.
- Example: Embracing setbacks as opportunities for learning and growth.

Long-Term Impact on Well-being
- The cumulative effect of positive habits extends to overall well-being.
- Sustained habits contribute to improved mental health, emotional resilience, and a sense of fulfillment.
- Example: Regular mindfulness practices enhancing emotional regulation and reducing stress.

Closing Thoughts

Sustaining positive habits for long-term success is a testament to your commitment to mindset mastery. Embrace the challenges, navigate through them with resilience, and celebrate each step of the journey. As you continue to cultivate positive habits, remember that the cumulative impact goes beyond individual actions, shaping not only your mindset but also the very fabric of your life.

Chapter 7
Gratitude and Positive Affirmations

Understanding the Psychology of Gratitude

"Ever wondered why a simple 'thank you' holds such power? Join me in unraveling the psychology of gratitude, an emotional treasure trove that can unlock the door to a mindset of abundance and fulfillment."

Gratitude Defined

Gratitude as an Emotion
- Gratitude is more than a polite gesture; it's a profound emotion.
- It involves recognizing and appreciating the positive aspects of life.
- Example: Feeling thankful for a supportive friend during challenging times.

Shift in Perspective
- Gratitude involves a shift from focusing on what's lacking to appreciating what's present.
- It's about acknowledging the good, even in the midst of difficulties.
- Example: Seeing the beauty in a rainy day instead of lamenting the lack of sunshine.

Explore the Psychological Benefits of Gratitude

"Imagine if there was a pill that could enhance your well-being and mindset. Well, it turns out, gratitude might be the closest thing to that magic elixir. Let's uncover the psychological benefits that gratitude brings into your life."

Positive Effects on Well-being

Enhanced Emotional Well-being
- Gratitude is linked to increased levels of positive emotions.
- Regular practice contributes to greater happiness and life satisfaction.
- Example: Noticing and appreciating small daily joys, like a warm cup of coffee or a beautiful sunset.

Reduced Stress and Anxiety
- Gratitude has a calming effect on the nervous system.
- Practicing gratitude can lead to lower levels of stress and anxiety.
- Example: Expressing gratitude for supportive relationships as a buffer against life's challenges.

Social Benefits

Improved Relationships
- Gratitude fosters a positive and appreciative atmosphere in relationships.
- Expressing gratitude strengthens social bonds and deepens connections.
- Example: Regularly expressing gratitude to a partner for their support and understanding.

Generosity and Altruism
- Grateful individuals tend to be more generous and altruistic.
- Gratitude promotes a desire to give back and contribute to the well-being of others.
- Example: Feeling grateful for personal growth and wanting to mentor others on a similar journey.

Discuss the Science Behind Gratitude and Brain Function

"Ready for a journey inside your brain? Let's explore the fascinating science behind gratitude and how it rewires your brain for positivity, resilience, and a mindset of abundance."

Neurological Impact

Gratitude and Dopamine

- Expressing gratitude triggers the release of dopamine, the brain's reward neurotransmitter.
- Dopamine reinforces the behavior of recognizing and appreciating positive experiences.
- Example: Keeping a gratitude journal leading to increased feelings of joy and fulfillment.

Effect on the Amygdala

- Gratitude has a calming effect on the amygdala, the brain's fear center.
- It reduces the activation of stress responses and promotes emotional regulation.
- Example: Practicing gratitude during challenging situations to mitigate the impact of stress.

Brain Plasticity and Rewiring

Neuroplasticity and Gratitude

- Regular gratitude practice contributes to neuroplasticity.
- The brain rewires itself, creating new neural pathways associated with positive thinking.
- Example: Cultivating a habit of gratitude leading to a more optimistic and resilient mindset.

Long-Term Impact on Brain Structure

- Prolonged gratitude practice may lead to changes in brain structure.
- The brain adapts to frequent positive thinking, influencing overall cognitive function.

- Example: Long-term gratitude practice associated with improved memory and cognitive flexibility.

Introduce the Concept of a Gratitude Journal

"What if you could capture the beauty of each day in words? Welcome to the world of a gratitude journal, your personal treasure chest for cultivating a mindset of abundance. Let's explore this simple yet powerful practice."

What is a Gratitude Journal?

A Daily Record of Blessings

- A gratitude journal is a place to record things you're thankful for each day.
- It serves as a tangible reminder of the positive aspects of life.
- Example: Writing down moments of joy, kindness, or personal achievements.

Cultivating Awareness

- The act of journaling encourages mindful reflection on daily experiences.
- It cultivates awareness of the abundance of positive elements in life.
- Example: Noticing and recording moments of gratitude, such as a kind gesture from a stranger.

Practical Tips for Gratitude Journaling

Consistency is Key

- Set a regular time for journaling, whether it's morning or evening.
- Consistency helps establish gratitude journaling as a positive habit.
- Example: Writing three things you're grateful for before bedtime.

Be Specific and Genuine

- Write specific details about what you're grateful for.
- Authenticity enhances the emotional impact of your entries.
- Example: Instead of "family," specify moments like a shared laughter-filled dinner.

Include Small and Big Moments

- Capture both significant and everyday moments of gratitude.
- Recognizing the beauty in small moments reinforces a positive mindset.

● Example: Expressing gratitude for a promotion at work and for a peaceful morning walk.

Closing Thoughts

Understanding the psychology of gratitude is like unlocking a treasure chest within yourself. As you delve into the emotional richness, recognize the power gratitude holds to shape your mindset, elevate your well-being, and rewire your brain for positivity. Through the simple practice of gratitude journaling, you can make this transformative journey a daily ritual, inviting abundance and fulfillment into every chapter of your life.

Creating a Positive Affirmation Practice

"Imagine having a secret weapon that can transform your thoughts, shape your beliefs, and set the stage for your mindset mastery journey. Welcome to the world of positive affirmations—a simple yet potent practice that can be your ally in unlocking your full potential."

Unveiling Positive Affirmations

What Are Positive Affirmations?

- Positive affirmations are short, positive statements aimed at shaping your mindset.
- They focus on desired traits, goals, or beliefs to cultivate a positive outlook.
- Example: "I am confident and capable of achieving my goals."

Daily Ritual of Affirmations

- Affirmations are most effective when practiced daily.
- Repetition helps embed positive beliefs into your subconscious mind.
- Example: Starting each day with a set of affirmations during morning routine.

Discuss the Role of Affirmations in Mindset Transformation

"Words have a powerful impact on our thoughts, and thoughts shape our reality. Let's dive into the transformative role of affirmations in rewiring your mindset, paving the way for a journey of self-discovery and empowerment."

The Power of Thoughts

Thoughts as Building Blocks of Reality

- Affirmations operate on the principle that thoughts shape actions and outcomes.

- Positive thoughts lead to positive actions, influencing your reality.

- Example: Affirming "I am resilient" fosters a mindset that tackles challenges with resilience.

Changing Negative Thought Patterns

- Affirmations serve as a tool to challenge and change negative thought patterns.

- By replacing negativity with positivity, they contribute to mindset transformation.

- Example: Shifting from "I can't do this" to "I am capable and resourceful."

Shaping Beliefs and Identity

Affirmations and Self-Identity

- Affirmations influence your self-identity by reinforcing positive beliefs.

- They contribute to a self-perception aligned with your goals and aspirations.

- Example: Affirming "I am worthy of success" reinforces a positive self-identity.

Building Confidence and Resilience

- Positive affirmations boost confidence and resilience.

- They create a foundation for facing challenges with a strong and positive mindset.

- Example: Repeating "I can handle whatever comes my way" enhances resilience.

Provide Guidelines for Crafting Powerful Affirmations

"Crafting affirmations is an art that transforms words into catalysts for change. Let's explore guidelines to ensure your affirmations pack a punch, resonating deeply with your subconscious mind."

Crafting Effective Affirmations

Be Positive and Present
- Formulate affirmations in the present tense and avoid negative phrasing.
- Positive, present-tense statements send a powerful message to the subconscious mind.
- Example: Instead of "I will overcome challenges," say "I overcome challenges with ease."

Keep it Specific and Concise
- Specific affirmations focus the mind on clear and achievable goals.
- Conciseness ensures easy recall and repetition.
- Example: "I am steadily advancing in my career" is more effective than a vague affirmation.

Use Vibrant and Descriptive Language
- Vibrant language evokes strong emotions and creates a vivid mental image.
- Descriptive affirmations enhance the emotional impact.
- Example: "I am radiating joy and gratitude in every aspect of my life."

Align with Core Values and Goals
- Affirmations should resonate with your core values and long-term goals.
- Alignment ensures authenticity and enhances their motivational impact.
- Example: Affirming "I am dedicated to continuous growth" aligns with a value for personal development.

Introduce the Use of Affirmations in Visualization

"What if you could step into a future where your aspirations are a reality? Enter the realm of affirmation visualization, where your mind paints the canvas of your desired outcomes, paving the way for manifestation and success."

Affirmations and Visualization

Enhancing Visualization with Affirmations
- Combining affirmations with visualization amplifies their impact.
- Visualization adds a sensory dimension, making affirmations more potent.
- Example: Visualizing career success while affirming "I am achieving my career goals."

Creating a Mental Movie
- Use affirmations to script a mental movie of your desired outcomes.
- This technique enhances the power of intention and belief.
- Example: Affirming "I am confident in public speaking" while visualizing a successful presentation.

Incorporating Affirmations into Daily Routine

Morning Affirmation Ritual
- Start your day with a set of affirmations.
- Morning affirmations set a positive tone for the day ahead.
- Example: Affirming "I am ready for the opportunities today brings" as part of your morning routine.

Affirmations Before Sleep
- Conclude your day with affirmations during bedtime.
- Bedtime affirmations influence the subconscious mind during sleep.
- Example: Affirming "I am grateful for the positive moments of today" before sleep.

Closing Thoughts

Creating a positive affirmation practice is like planting seeds of empowerment in the garden of your mind. As you craft and embrace affirmations, remember that the journey toward mindset mastery is a gradual, transformative process. Affirmations, when woven into your daily routine with sincerity and consistency, can be the guiding stars that lead you toward the full realization of your potential.

Expressing Gratitude in Relationships

"Picture your relationships as gardens—lush, vibrant, and filled with the beauty of connection. Let's explore how the simple act of expressing gratitude can be the sunlight and water that nourish these gardens, fostering growth, harmony, and lasting bonds."

The Art of Expressing Gratitude

Why Expressing Gratitude Matters

- Expressing gratitude is a way of acknowledging and valuing the people in your life.
- It adds a layer of warmth, kindness, and appreciation to relationships.
- Example: A heartfelt "thank you" for a supportive friend enhances the bond between you.

Gratitude as a Two-Way Street

- Expressing gratitude not only uplifts others but also contributes to your own sense of well-being.
- It creates a positive cycle of mutual appreciation within relationships.
- Example: Feeling joy when expressing gratitude reinforces the act of expressing it more frequently.

Explore the Impact of Gratitude on Interpersonal Relationships

"Imagine if every relationship had a secret ingredient that made it stronger, more resilient, and filled with positivity. That secret ingredient? Gratitude. Let's delve into the profound impact gratitude has on the dynamics of interpersonal connections."

Strengthening Connection

Building Trust and Connection

- Gratitude builds a foundation of trust and deepens the emotional connection.
- It fosters an environment where individuals feel seen and valued.
- Example: Regular expressions of gratitude create a sense of security in relationships.

Positive Influence on Communication

- Gratitude positively influences the tone and quality of communication.
- It encourages open and honest dialogue, reducing misunderstandings.
- Example: Expressing gratitude for effective communication strengthens the communication channels.

Fostering Emotional Resilience

Enhancing Emotional Resilience

- Gratitude acts as a buffer during challenging times.
- It provides a reservoir of positive emotions that can be drawn upon in difficult situations.
- Example: In times of stress, recalling moments of gratitude can bring emotional relief.

Creating a Supportive Atmosphere

- Gratitude creates an atmosphere of support and encouragement.
- It reinforces the idea that individuals are there for each other.
- Example: Expressing gratitude for a partner's efforts fosters a supportive environment.

Discuss the Role of Appreciation in Fostering Connection

"In the grand symphony of relationships, appreciation plays a melody that resonates deeply, creating harmony and strengthening the bonds that tie us together. Let's explore the vital role of appreciation in nurturing connection."

The Importance of Appreciation

Acknowledging Efforts and Contributions

- Appreciation is about recognizing and acknowledging the efforts and contributions of others.
- It validates the value each person brings to the relationship.
- Example: Expressing appreciation for a colleague's hard work boosts morale.

Fostering a Positive Environment

- Appreciation contributes to a positive and uplifting environment.
- It creates a culture where positivity and gratitude become the norm.
- Example: A workplace where appreciation is freely expressed promotes a positive work culture.

Building a Culture of Gratitude

Regular Expressions of Appreciation

- Consistent expressions of appreciation build a culture of gratitude.
- It becomes a part of the relationship's fabric, influencing daily interactions.
- Example: Regularly appreciating family members for their contributions to household chores.

Encouraging Growth and Development

- Appreciation fosters an environment where individuals feel encouraged to grow.
- It provides positive reinforcement for personal and professional development.
- Example: Acknowledging a friend's personal growth journey and expressing appreciation for their efforts.

Provide Actionable Steps for Expressing Gratitude

"Ready to infuse your relationships with the magic of gratitude? Let's uncover practical and simple steps that you can take today to express gratitude in a way that resonates, creating ripples of positivity in your personal and professional connections."

Simple Acts of Gratitude

Verbal Expressions

- Vocalize your appreciation through simple phrases like "thank you" or "I appreciate you."
- Verbal expressions carry sincerity and have an immediate positive impact.
- Example: Saying "thank you" to a friend for lending a listening ear.

Handwritten Notes or Messages

- Penning down your gratitude in a handwritten note adds a personal touch.
- It allows for reflection and provides a tangible reminder of appreciation.
- Example: Writing a heartfelt note to a family member for their continuous support.

Acts of Service

Offering Help and Support

- Acts of service demonstrate your appreciation through actions.
- It can be as simple as helping with tasks or offering support during challenging times.
- Example: Helping a colleague with their workload during a busy period.

Surprise Gestures

- Surprising someone with a thoughtful gesture shows that you value and appreciate them.
- Thoughtful surprises can range from a small gift to planning a special day.
- Example: Sending flowers or a handwritten note to express gratitude to a friend.

Cultivating Gratitude Rituals

Gratitude Journaling Together
- Share a gratitude journal with a friend or partner.
- Each day, jot down things you appreciate about each other.
- Example: Reflecting on shared moments and expressing gratitude for the positive aspects of the relationship.

Gratitude Rituals in the Workplace
- Introduce gratitude rituals in the workplace, such as a weekly appreciation session.
- Encourage colleagues to express gratitude for each other's contributions.
- Example: Taking a moment during team meetings to acknowledge and appreciate team members.

Closing Thoughts

Expressing gratitude in relationships is a transformative practice that enriches the soil of connection, allowing the bonds to grow deeper and stronger. As you embark on this journey of cultivating gratitude in your relationships, remember that small, sincere gestures can have a significant impact. Whether through words, actions, or shared rituals, the magic of gratitude lies in its simplicity and authenticity, creating a tapestry of connection that elevates every relationship in your life.

Overcoming Negativity Bias with Positivity

"Imagine your mind as a garden where thoughts bloom. Let's explore the persistent weeds of negativity and how, with the sunlight of positivity, you can cultivate a mindset that blossoms with resilience, optimism, and the full potential of your being."

Understanding Negativity Bias

The Tug of Negativity

- Negativity bias is a psychological phenomenon where the mind is more influenced by negative stimuli than positive ones.
- It's an evolutionary trait designed to prioritize potential threats for survival.
- Example: Remembering a single criticism amidst a sea of compliments.

Impact on Emotional Landscape

- Negativity bias influences emotions, leading to a disproportionate focus on negative experiences.
- This bias can contribute to stress, anxiety, and a generally pessimistic outlook.
- Example: Dwelling on a minor setback while overlooking significant achievements.

Discuss the Negativity Bias and Its Impact on Mindset

"In the journey of mindset mastery, understanding the enemy is crucial. Let's unravel the intricacies of negativity bias and its profound impact on shaping the lens through which we view the world."

The Power of Negative Thoughts

Sticky Nature of Negative Thoughts

- Negative thoughts tend to stick in the mind more readily than positive ones.
- This stickiness can lead to rumination, reinforcing the negativity bias.
- Example: Replaying a perceived failure repeatedly in your mind.

Influence on Decision-Making

- Negativity bias can influence decision-making, prompting cautious or risk-averse choices.
- It can hinder seizing opportunities due to an exaggerated fear of negative outcomes.
- Example: Avoiding a new endeavor due to fear of potential failure.

Shaping Mindset and Perspectives

Pervasive Impact on Mindset

- Negativity bias contributes to the formation of a negative mindset.
- It shapes how one interprets events, relationships, and personal experiences.
- Example: Interpreting a neutral comment as criticism due to the influence of negativity bias.

Implications for Self-Esteem

- Constant exposure to negativity can impact self-esteem and self-worth.
- It may create a distorted self-perception, focusing on perceived shortcomings.
- Example: Believing you are not good enough despite evidence of competence.

Provide Strategies for Overcoming Negativity Bias

"Breaking free from the shackles of negativity requires strategic intervention. Let's explore practical and accessible strategies to loosen the grip of negativity bias, allowing positivity to take center stage in your mental landscape."

Strategies for Overcoming Negativity Bias

Cultivating Awareness

- Developing mindfulness and awareness helps identify negative thought patterns.
- Recognizing when negativity arises is the first step toward overcoming it.
- Example: Noticing self-critical thoughts during moments of stress.

Balancing Perspectives

- Actively seek out positive aspects in situations where negativity bias is prevalent.
- Balance negative thoughts with positive ones to create a more accurate perception.
- Example: Acknowledging accomplishments alongside perceived failures.

Gratitude Practice

- Engaging in regular gratitude practices counters negativity bias by focusing on positive aspects.
- Listing things to be grateful for shifts the focus away from negative thoughts.
- Example: Expressing gratitude for small daily joys to counterbalance negativity.

Mindful Reframing

- Reframe negative thoughts by consciously challenging and altering them.
- Replace irrational or negative beliefs with more balanced and positive ones.
- Example: Transforming "I can't do this" to "I'll do my best and learn from the experience."

Explore the Role of Positive Affirmations in Challenging Negative Thoughts

"In the battle of the mind, positive affirmations emerge as powerful allies. Let's explore how these simple yet profound statements can challenge the stronghold of negative thoughts, paving the way for a mindset of resilience and self-belief."

The Power of Positive Affirmations

Counteracting Negative Self-Talk

- Positive affirmations act as a direct counter to negative self-talk.
- They challenge and replace destructive thoughts with constructive and empowering ones.
- Example: Affirming "I am capable and resilient" to challenge feelings of inadequacy.

Shaping Positive Beliefs

- Regular use of positive affirmations shapes positive beliefs about oneself.
- Over time, these affirmations contribute to a more optimistic and confident mindset.
- Example: Affirming "I am worthy of success" to foster a belief in one's capabilities.

Incorporating Positive Affirmations into Daily Life

Morning Affirmation Ritual

- Start the day with a set of positive affirmations to set a positive tone.
- Morning affirmations influence mindset throughout the day.
- Example: Affirming "Today, I choose joy and positivity" each morning.

Affirmations During Challenging Moments

- Use affirmations during moments of stress or self-doubt.
- They serve as a tool to recenter and challenge negative thoughts in real-time.
- Example: Affirming "I am resilient; I can handle this challenge" during a difficult task.

Closing Thoughts

Overcoming negativity bias with positivity is a transformative journey toward mindset mastery. As you implement strategies to loosen the grip of negativity and embrace the power of positive affirmations, remember that small, consistent steps yield significant results. By cultivating awareness, balancing perspectives, and infusing your daily life with positivity, you can reshape the landscape of your mind, allowing the seeds of resilience and optimism to flourish and unleash your full potential.

Gratitude as a Lifestyle

"Picture a life where gratitude is not just a practice but a guiding force—a lifestyle that transforms how you perceive and interact with the world. Let's embark on a journey into the heart of gratitude, exploring how it can become an integral part of your everyday existence."

The Essence of Gratitude as a Lifestyle

Moving Beyond a Practice

- Gratitude as a lifestyle transcends occasional acts of thankfulness.

- It becomes an inherent part of your daily interactions, thoughts, and overall outlook.

- Example: Infusing gratitude into routine activities like meals, conversations, and reflective moments.

Mindset Shift

- Adopting gratitude as a lifestyle involves a fundamental shift in mindset.

- It's about cultivating a perpetual state of appreciation and recognizing the positive aspects of life.

- Example: Finding joy in simple pleasures, from the warmth of sunlight to the laughter of loved ones.

Discuss the Transition from Occasional Practice to a Lifestyle of Gratitude

"Changing habits can be like navigating a winding road. Let's explore the twists and turns of transitioning from sporadic acts of gratitude to seamlessly integrating this transformative mindset into the fabric of your daily life."

Gradual Integration

Consistency in Practice

- The transition begins with consistent and intentional gratitude practices.
- Regular expressions of thankfulness lay the foundation for a shift in lifestyle.
- Example: Daily journaling or reflecting on three things to be grateful for.

Incorporating Gratitude into Routine

- Integrate gratitude into daily routines, making it a natural part of your day.
- This includes morning reflections, mealtime appreciations, or bedtime gratitude.
- Example: Expressing thanks before meals and reflecting on positive moments before sleep.

Cultivating a Gratitude Mindset

Internalizing the Mindset Shift

- Over time, occasional gratitude practices evolve into a broader mindset shift.
- Gratitude becomes an automatic response, influencing how you perceive challenges and triumphs.
- Example: Reacting to setbacks with a mindset of learning and growth.

Expanding the Circle of Gratitude

- Transitioning to a gratitude lifestyle involves extending appreciation to various aspects of life.
- It's not limited to personal achievements but includes nature, relationships, and experiences.

- Example: Expressing gratitude for the support of friends, the beauty of nature, or opportunities for growth.

Share Stories of Individuals Transformed by a Gratitude Mindset

"Witness the profound impact of gratitude through real stories of individuals whose lives have been touched, transformed, and enriched by embracing gratitude as a guiding light. These stories serve as beacons, illuminating the transformative power of a grateful heart."

Stories of Transformation

Overcoming Adversity

- Share stories of individuals who navigated challenges with a gratitude mindset.
- Gratitude served as a source of resilience and a catalyst for positive change.
- Example: A person finding gratitude amidst health challenges, focusing on moments of joy and support.

Fostering Connection and Joy

- Narrate experiences where gratitude strengthened relationships and brought joy.
- Grateful individuals often radiate positivity, creating a ripple effect in their communities.
- Example: A family brought closer together by expressing mutual appreciation regularly.

Lessons from Transformation

Shift in Perspective

- Highlight how adopting a gratitude lifestyle resulted in a profound shift in perspective.
- Gratitude became a lens through which individuals viewed their lives, emphasizing the positive.
- Example: Seeing setbacks as opportunities for growth and learning.

Enhanced Well-Being

• Explore how gratitude contributed to improved mental and emotional well-being.

• Stories could include individuals experiencing reduced stress, increased happiness, and a greater sense of fulfillment.

• Example: A person finding peace and contentment through a daily gratitude practice.

Provide Practical Tips for Maintaining a Grateful Perspective

"Elevate your gratitude lifestyle with practical tips that ensure this transformative mindset becomes a constant companion in your journey towards mindset mastery. These simple yet effective strategies are the stepping stones to a life illuminated by the warmth of gratitude."

Practical Tips for a Grateful Lifestyle

Gratitude Journaling

- Maintain a gratitude journal to record daily moments of thankfulness.
- Reflecting on positive experiences reinforces a grateful mindset.
- Example: List three things you're grateful for each day.

Mindful Appreciation

- Practice mindful appreciation during routine activities.
- Engage all your senses in the experience, deepening the impact of gratitude.
- Example: Fully savoring the flavors of a meal or appreciating the beauty of nature during a walk.

Expressing Gratitude to Others

- Verbalize your gratitude to friends, family, and colleagues.
- Expressing appreciation strengthens relationships and creates a positive atmosphere.
- Example: Sending a heartfelt thank-you message or note.

Gratitude Reminders

- Set reminders throughout the day to pause and express gratitude.
- These brief moments of reflection reinforce a grateful perspective.
- Example: Setting alarms on your phone with positive affirmations or gratitude prompts.

Gratitude Challenges

- Engage in gratitude challenges with friends or online communities.
- Sharing your daily expressions of gratitude fosters a sense of accountability and community.

- Example: Participating in a 30-day gratitude challenge.

Closing Thoughts

Gratitude as a lifestyle is a transformative journey—one that unfolds with consistent practice, a shift in mindset, and the weaving of gratitude into the very fabric of your daily existence. As you explore the stories of those touched by gratitude and embrace practical tips, remember that this is not just a practice; it's a way of being. The path to mindset mastery is illuminated by the radiant glow of a grateful heart, guiding you towards the full realization of your limitless potential.

Chapter 8
Mindful Decision Making

Understanding Decision-Making Processes

"Life is a series of choices, each one shaping the path we walk. Let's delve into the intricate world of decision-making, unraveling the threads that weave our choices and exploring how mastering this art can be the key to unlocking your full potential."

The Complexity of Decision-Making

Decision-Making as a Daily Art

● Every day, we encounter a myriad of decisions, from the mundane to the life-altering.

● Understanding the underlying processes behind decision-making is crucial for intentional living.

● Example: Choosing what to wear or deciding on a career path—both involve decision-making.

Impact on Mindset

● Our choices contribute to the formation of our mindset.

● The quality of decisions influences our sense of control, confidence, and overall well-being.

● Example: Positive decision-making fosters a growth mindset, while negative choices may lead to self-doubt.

Discuss the Cognitive Processes Involved in Decision-Making

"Ever wonder what goes on inside your mind when faced with a decision? Let's pull back the curtain and explore the cognitive processes that shape our choices, providing insights into the mysterious world of decision-making."

Stages of Decision-Making

Identification of the Decision

- The process begins with recognizing that a decision needs to be made.
- It involves defining the problem or opportunity that requires a choice.
- Example: Recognizing the need to choose a career path after graduation.

Gathering Information

- Decision-making involves collecting relevant information.
- This stage requires seeking facts, opinions, and insights to inform the choice.
- Example: Researching different career options, potential salaries, and job satisfaction.

Evaluation of Options

- Individuals assess the available options based on gathered information.
- This stage involves weighing the pros and cons of each choice.
- Example: Considering the alignment of a career with personal values, skills, and interests.

Decision-Making and Commitment

- The final stage is making the decision and committing to the chosen option.
- This step involves a blend of rational analysis and intuition.
- Example: Choosing a specific career path and committing to pursuing it.

Influences on Decision-Making

Cognitive Biases

- Cognitive biases, such as confirmation bias or anchoring, can subtly influence decisions.

- These biases stem from mental shortcuts that may lead to less-than-optimal choices.

- Example: Confirming pre-existing beliefs rather than objectively evaluating new information.

Social and Cultural Influences

- Social and cultural factors play a significant role in decision-making.

- Expectations from family, peers, and societal norms can shape choices.

- Example: Pursuing a particular career due to family expectations or cultural norms.

Explore the Impact of Emotions on Choices

"Emotions are silent architects of our decisions, painting our choices with hues of joy, fear, or excitement. Let's embark on an emotional journey within decision-making, uncovering how feelings shape the paths we choose to tread."

Emotional Influences on Decisions

The Emotional Palette of Choices

- Emotions are integral to decision-making, coloring choices with feelings of happiness, anxiety, or anticipation.
- The emotional context surrounding a decision significantly impacts the perceived outcomes.
- Example: Choosing a career out of passion and excitement rather than solely for financial gain.

Fear and Decision Avoidance

- Fear can hinder decision-making, leading to avoidance or indecision.
- Negative emotions, if not managed, may paralyze the ability to make choices.
- Example: Avoiding a career change due to fear of the unknown or fear of failure.

Emotional Intelligence in Decision-Making

Awareness and Regulation of Emotions

- Emotional intelligence involves recognizing and managing emotions during decision-making.
- Emotionally intelligent individuals can navigate choices with clarity and self-awareness.
- Example: Acknowledging anxiety about a decision and employing strategies to manage and regulate it.

Aligning Emotions with Values

- A harmonious decision aligns emotional responses with personal values.
- This alignment enhances satisfaction and fulfillment in the chosen path.

- Example: Feeling a deep sense of fulfillment when a decision aligns with personal values and aspirations.

Introduce the Concept of Decision Fatigue

"Ever felt mentally drained after a series of decisions, as if your brain's batteries were running low? Let's unravel the concept of decision fatigue, exploring how the wear and tear on our mental faculties can impact the choices we make."

Understanding Decision Fatigue

Depletion of Mental Resources

- Decision fatigue occurs when the mental energy required for decision-making is depleted.
- The more decisions made, the less cognitive resources are available for subsequent choices.
- Example: Feeling exhausted after making numerous small decisions throughout the day.

Impact on Decision Quality

- Decision fatigue can lead to suboptimal choices, as cognitive resources diminish.
- Individuals may resort to shortcuts or impulsivity when experiencing decision fatigue.
- Example: Opting for unhealthy food choices when too fatigued to make thoughtful decisions about meals.

Mitigating Decision Fatigue

Prioritizing Key Decisions

- Recognizing the limited cognitive bandwidth, prioritize significant decisions.
- Reserve mental energy for choices that align with long-term goals and values.
- Example: Allocating focused decision-making time for career-related choices.

Creating Decision-Making Routines

● Establishing routines for repetitive or minor decisions minimizes decision fatigue.

● Streamlining choices in certain areas allows for greater mental clarity in other domains.

● Example: Adopting a consistent morning routine to reduce decision fatigue related to clothing choices.

Closing Thoughts

Understanding the intricacies of decision-making unveils the artistry behind the choices that shape our lives. From the cognitive processes that guide our reasoning to the emotional palette that colors our decisions, and the subtle fatigue that affects our choices—mastering decision-making is a cornerstone of mindset mastery. As you navigate the crossroads of life, may the insights into decision-making empower you to embrace a path aligned with your full potential, enriching your journey toward mindset mastery.

Mindful Decision-Making Techniques

"Ever felt overwhelmed by decisions, unsure which path to take? Let's explore the art of mindful decision-making—a journey that transforms choices into opportunities for growth, clarity, and alignment with your authentic self."

Introduce Mindfulness Techniques for Decision-Making

The Power of Presence

- Mindfulness in decision-making begins with being fully present in the moment.
- Grounding yourself in the now helps to cut through distractions and external pressures.
- *Example: Imagine making a decision with a clear mind, free from past regrets or future anxieties.*

Cultivating Non-Judgmental Awareness

- Mindfulness encourages observing thoughts without judgment.
- Detaching from preconceived notions allows for a more objective evaluation of choices.
- *Example: Imagine considering a career change without labeling past decisions as 'good' or 'bad.'*

Embracing Open-Mindedness

- Mindful decision-making involves approaching choices with openness.
- Embracing a curious and receptive mindset facilitates exploration of diverse possibilities.
- *Example: Consider approaching a challenging decision with the openness of a beginner's mind.*

Discuss the Importance of Clarity in Decision-Making

"In the fog of indecision, clarity becomes the guiding light. Let's unravel the importance of clarity in decision-making, understanding how a clear mind can transform complex choices into opportunities for growth and fulfillment."

The Role of Clarity

Cutting Through Confusion

- Clarity is the beacon that cuts through the fog of uncertainty.
- A clear mind helps in understanding the nuances of a decision.
- *Example: Picture a decision-making process where confusion dissipates, leaving a clear path.*

Alignment with Values

- Clarity allows for a deeper understanding of personal values.
- Decisions made in alignment with core values are more likely to lead to satisfaction.
- *Example: Visualize making a decision that resonates with your deepest values and principles.*

Provide a Step-by-Step Guide to Mindful Decision-Making

"Embarking on a mindful decision-making journey requires a roadmap. Let's navigate this path step by step, unveiling a guide that transforms choices into conscious and intentional steps towards your full potential."

Step 1: Pause and Breathe

- Before diving into decision-making, take a moment to pause and breathe.
  - Mindful breathing calms the mind and anchors you in the present moment.
  - *Example: Imagine taking a deep breath before considering a significant life choice.*

Step 2: Clarify Your Intention

- Clearly define your intention behind the decision.
  - This step ensures that your choices align with your overarching goals and aspirations.
  - *Example: Reflect on the intention behind choosing a particular career path—seeking passion, financial stability, or personal growth.*

Step 3: Gather Information Mindfully

- Approach the gathering of information with mindfulness.
  - Be aware of biases and maintain an open mind during research and exploration.
  - *Example: Imagine researching potential options without being swayed by external opinions or biases.*

Step 4: Observe Your Emotions

- Pay attention to the emotions arising during the decision-making process.
  - Mindful observation allows for understanding and managing emotional influences.

- *Example: Recognize feelings of fear or excitement when contemplating a significant life change.*

Step 5: Evaluate Options Non-Judgmentally

- Evaluate options without judgment or attachment.
  - Detaching from preconceived notions fosters a more objective assessment.
  - *Example: Consider the pros and cons of different career paths without labeling them as 'good' or 'bad.'*

Step 6: Consult Your Inner Wisdom

- Connect with your inner wisdom or intuition.
  - Trusting your instincts contributes to a more authentic decision-making process.
  - *Example: Picture listening to your gut feeling when faced with a choice that aligns with your true self.*

Step 7: Make the Decision Mindfully

- Finally, make the decision with mindfulness.
  - Approach the choice with the full awareness of its implications and alignment with your intention.
  - *Example: Envision making a decision confidently, knowing it resonates with your values and aspirations.*

Closing Thoughts

Mindful decision-making is not just a process; it's a transformative journey where choices become opportunities for growth, alignment, and self-discovery. As you embark on the path of mindful decision-making, may each choice become a conscious step toward unlocking your full potential. Remember, clarity and mindfulness are your companions on this journey, guiding you toward a mindset mastery that empowers you to shape a life in harmony with your authentic self.

Overcoming Decision Paralysis

"Ever found yourself stuck in the quagmire of indecision, unable to choose a path forward? Let's unravel the mystery of decision paralysis—a common hurdle on the journey to mindset mastery—and explore strategies to break free from its grip."

Discuss Common Challenges Leading to Decision Paralysis

Fear of Making the Wrong Choice
- The fear of making a wrong decision can paralyze individuals.
- This fear often stems from a misconception that there is only one 'right' path.
- *Example: Imagine the weight of choosing a career, fearing it might be the wrong one.*

Overwhelm from Too Many Options
- An abundance of choices can overwhelm and hinder decision-making.
- The paradox of choice can lead to analysis paralysis, making decisions seem insurmountable.
- *Example: Visualize standing in a grocery aisle with countless options, struggling to pick one product.*

Perfectionism
- A desire for perfection can immobilize decision-making.
- The unrealistic pursuit of a perfect choice creates a mental gridlock.
- *Example: Consider the pressure of choosing the perfect vacation spot, fearing any imperfection.*

External Pressures and Expectations
- External expectations from society, family, or peers can contribute to indecision.
- The weight of meeting others' expectations can lead to a fear of disappointing.
- *Example: Envision the challenge of choosing a career that aligns with personal passion versus societal expectations.*

Provide Strategies for Overcoming Indecision

"Breaking free from decision paralysis requires a toolbox of strategies. Let's dive into practical approaches to untangle the knots of indecision, empowering you to make choices with clarity and confidence."

Strategy 1: Set Realistic Expectations

- Acknowledge that perfection is an illusion.
  - Embrace the idea that decisions are rarely irreversible, allowing for learning and adaptation.
  - *Example: Recognize that the perfect career may not exist, but each choice contributes to personal growth.*

Strategy 2: Limit Choices

- Simplify decisions by narrowing down options.
  - Establish criteria for choices, focusing on key factors that align with your values.
  - *Example: When choosing a restaurant, narrow down options based on cuisine preference and location.*

Strategy 3: Break It Down

- Divide complex decisions into smaller, more manageable tasks.
  - Tackling decisions incrementally reduces the perceived enormity.
  - *Example: Instead of deciding on a whole career change at once, break it down into steps like skill-building or informational interviews.*

Strategy 4: Accept Imperfection

- Embrace the imperfections inherent in decision-making.
  - Understand that outcomes may not always match expectations, and that's okay.
  - *Example: Realize that a vacation may have unexpected challenges, but these can become part of the adventure.*

Explore the Role of Mindset in Breaking Decision-Making Patterns

"Unveiling the power of mindset in overcoming decision paralysis is like discovering a hidden key to unlock the door to your potential. Let's delve into the profound impact of mindset on breaking free from patterns of indecision."

Cultivate a Growth Mindset

● A growth mindset views challenges as opportunities for learning and growth.

● Embrace the belief that decisions, whether 'right' or 'wrong,' contribute to personal development.

● *Example: Instead of seeing a career setback as a failure, view it as a chance to learn and pivot.*

Develop Self-Compassion

● Practice self-compassion when facing indecision.

● Understand that everyone makes imperfect choices, and it's part of the shared human experience.

● *Example: Instead of self-criticism for a seemingly wrong decision, offer yourself understanding and kindness.*

Shift from Fixed to Open Mindset

● Move away from a fixed mindset that demands a 'perfect' choice.

● Embrace an open mindset that values the journey, where decisions contribute to a dynamic life story.

● *Example: Instead of fixating on a 'perfect' relationship, appreciate the growth and lessons each one brings.*

Embrace the Power of Decisiveness

● Cultivate a mindset that values decisiveness as a strength.

● See making choices as a proactive step toward progress, even if they are not flawless.

● *Example: Celebrate the courage it takes to decide and take action, regardless of the outcome.*

Closing Thoughts

Decision paralysis, with its web of challenges, is a universal experience. By understanding the common pitfalls and employing practical strategies, you can navigate the maze of indecision. Embracing a mindset that values growth, imperfection, and decisiveness is the key to breaking free from patterns that hinder your journey to mindset mastery. As you embark on this transformative path, may each decision become an opportunity to sculpt a mindset that empowers you to unleash your full potential.

Aligning Decisions with Values and Goals

"Ever felt adrift, making decisions without a compass? Let's embark on a journey to discover the transformative power of aligning decisions with your values and goals—a path that ensures each choice propels you closer to your full potential."

Explore the Importance of Aligning Decisions with Personal Values

The Guiding Light of Values

● Personal values act as a compass, providing direction in decision-making.

● Aligning choices with core values enhances a sense of authenticity and fulfillment.

● *Example: Picture making a career decision that resonates with your fundamental values, bringing a sense of purpose.*

Avoiding the Divergence Dilemma

● Misaligned decisions can lead to internal conflicts and a sense of being off-course.

● Aligning choices with values minimizes the internal struggle that arises from conflicting decisions.

● *Example: Imagine the harmony of choosing a life partner whose values align with yours, reducing potential conflicts.*

Building a Cohesive Life Narrative

● Aligned decisions contribute to a cohesive life narrative.

● Each choice becomes a chapter that fits seamlessly into the overarching story of your life.

● *Example: Visualize a decision-making journey where each chapter builds upon the last, creating a meaningful life story.*

Discuss the Role of Goals in Guiding Decision-Making

"Setting sail without a destination leads to aimless wandering. Let's uncover the significance of goals in steering your decision-making ship, ensuring each choice aligns with the course you've set for yourself."

Goals as Decision-Making Anchors

- Goals serve as anchors, grounding decisions in a broader context.
- Aligning choices with goals ensures they contribute to the larger vision for your life.
- *Example: Picture making daily choices that inch you closer to a health goal, contributing to a vibrant life.*

Creating a Roadmap for Progress

- Goals provide a roadmap, offering a sense of purpose and direction.
- Decision alignment with goals transforms choices into intentional steps toward progress.
- *Example: Envision setting a goal for career advancement, and each decision made contributes to the upward trajectory.*

Mitigating Decision Overwhelm

- Clear goals simplify decision-making by filtering choices through a predefined lens.
- When decisions align with goals, the array of choices becomes more manageable.
- *Example: Imagine navigating a complex decision by evaluating options based on their alignment with your overarching life goals.*

Provide Exercises for Clarifying Values and Setting Decision Criteria

"Ready to chart the course of alignment? Let's engage in practical exercises that will crystalize your values and establish decision criteria, ensuring that your choices resonate with your true self and propel you toward your desired future."

Exercise 1: Values Clarification

Steps:

List Your Core Values
- Jot down values that are fundamental to who you are.
- *Example: Integrity, family, growth, compassion.*

Prioritize Your Values
- Arrange the values in order of importance.
- *Example: Identify which values hold the most significance for you.*

Reflect on Past Decisions
- Consider past decisions and evaluate how well they aligned with your identified values.
- *Example: Ponder how choosing a certain job aligned with your prioritized values.*

Exercise 2: Goal Setting and Decision Criteria

Steps:

Define Short and Long-Term Goals
- Outline both short-term and long-term goals for different aspects of your life.
- *Example: Short-term goal - Improve physical fitness; Long-term goal - Establish a successful career.*

Establish Decision Criteria

- Identify criteria that align with your goals to evaluate potential choices.
- *Example: Decision criteria for career choices - align with long-term career goals, provide opportunities for growth.*

Regularly Review and Adjust

- Periodically review your goals and decision criteria, adjusting them as your priorities evolve.
- *Example: Reassess your fitness goals and adjust your workout routine as needed.*

Closing Thoughts

Aligning decisions with values and goals is the compass that guides you through the vast sea of choices. As you embark on this journey of intentional decision-making, may each choice echo with authenticity and purpose, propelling you steadily toward mindset mastery and the fulfillment of your full potential. Remember, the power to shape your destiny lies in the alignment of your choices with the values and goals that define the essence of who you are and where you aspire to be.

Learning from Decisions, Whether Positive or Negative

"Decisions—some lead to triumphs, others to setbacks. Let's unravel the art of learning from every choice, transforming both victories and defeats into stepping stones on your path to mindset mastery and unlocking your full potential."

Discuss the Value of Learning from Both Successful and Failed Decisions

Triumphs: Celebrating Success

- Successful decisions provide a sense of accomplishment and validation.
- Celebrating victories reinforces positive behavior and boosts confidence.
- *Example: Imagine the satisfaction of making a career move that leads to a fulfilling job and professional growth.*

Setbacks: The Hidden Gems of Growth

- Failed decisions offer invaluable lessons and opportunities for growth.
- Embracing setbacks cultivates resilience and a mindset of learning.
- *Example: Picture the resilience developed after a failed business venture, leading to insights for future success.*

Shifting Perspectives on Failure

- Reframe the concept of failure as a necessary component of success.
- Failure becomes a teacher, guiding individuals toward improved decision-making.
- *Example: Visualize seeing a relationship ending not as a failure but as a lesson in understanding personal needs and priorities.*

Explore the Mindset of Continuous Improvement

"In the realm of mindset mastery, the journey is as vital as the destination. Let's delve into the transformative power of a mindset rooted in continuous improvement—a mindset that turns every decision, good or bad, into a stepping stone for growth."

The Growth Mindset

● Embrace a growth mindset that sees challenges as opportunities for learning.

● Every decision becomes a chance to improve and develop resilience.

● *Example: Envision approaching a challenging project with enthusiasm, viewing obstacles as chances to develop new skills.*

Resilience as a Skill

● Cultivate resilience as a skill honed through continuous improvement.

● Resilience enables bouncing back from setbacks and maintaining a positive outlook.

● *Example: Consider the resilience built after facing rejection, emerging stronger and more determined in subsequent pursuits.*

The Iterative Nature of Decision-Making

● Recognize that decision-making is an iterative process of improvement.

● Each choice informs the next, creating a cycle of growth and refinement.

● *Example: Picture refining your approach to time management after recognizing past inefficiencies.*

Provide Reflective Exercises to Extract Lessons from Past Decisions

"Ready to unlock the wisdom embedded in your past decisions? Engage in reflective exercises designed to extract valuable lessons, turning every choice into a source of insight and empowerment."

Exercise 1: The Success Reflection

Steps:

Identify a Recent Success
- Choose a recent decision that resulted in a positive outcome.
- *Example: Recall a successful collaboration at work.*

Deconstruct the Decision
- Break down the decision into its components.
- *Example: Identify the factors that contributed to the successful collaboration, such as effective communication and teamwork.*

Reflect on Personal Growth
- Consider how this success contributed to personal growth.
- *Example: Recognize improved communication skills and the ability to collaborate effectively.*

Exercise 2: The Setback Analysis

Steps:

Select a Setback
- Choose a decision that did not go as planned.
- *Example: Reflect on a failed project or missed opportunity.*

Identify Contributing Factors
- Analyze factors that contributed to the setback.
- *Example: Explore aspects such as lack of preparation or unforeseen challenges.*

Extract Lessons Learned
- Identify specific lessons learned from the setback.
- *Example: Learnings may include the importance of contingency planning or the need for additional skills.*

Exercise 3: Continuous Improvement Action Plan

Steps:

Set Improvement Goals
- Establish specific areas for improvement based on past reflections.
- *Example: Set a goal to enhance decision-making by seeking additional training or mentorship.*

Create a Learning Schedule
- Develop a schedule for continuous learning and improvement.
- *Example: Dedicate time each week to reading relevant literature, attending workshops, or engaging in skill-building activities.*

Track Progress
- Regularly assess progress toward improvement goals.
- *Example: Monitor enhanced decision-making skills and celebrate small victories along the way.*

Closing Thoughts

Learning from decisions, whether positive or negative, is the cornerstone of mindset mastery. Every choice is a chance to celebrate success, embrace setbacks as opportunities for growth, and continually refine your approach to decision-making. As you engage in reflective exercises and cultivate a mindset of continuous improvement, may each decision become a beacon guiding you toward unlocking your full potential and achieving mastery over your mindset. Remember, the journey of growth is threaded with the lessons drawn from every step you take.

Understanding the Relationship-Mindset Connection

"Ever wondered how the people around you influence the way you think and feel? Let's dive into the intriguing world of the relationship-mindset connection—a dynamic interplay that shapes your thoughts, feelings, and ultimately, your journey to mindset mastery."

Explore the Reciprocal Influence of Relationships and Mindset

The Mirror Effect

- Relationships act as mirrors, reflecting and shaping our mindset.
- Positive interactions can uplift and reinforce a growth-oriented mindset.
- *Example: Imagine being surrounded by friends who encourage your dreams, reinforcing a mindset of ambition and possibility.*

Mindset Contagion

- Mindsets are contagious, spreading through social interactions.
- Positive mindsets can inspire those around us, fostering a supportive environment.
- *Example: Consider how a colleague's optimistic outlook can influence the team, creating a positive and collaborative atmosphere.*

The Power of Collective Mindset

- Collective mindsets within a group influence individual perspectives.
- Being part of a growth-oriented community nurtures and amplifies individual mindsets.
- *Example: Picture a family that values continuous learning; each member is likely to adopt a mindset of curiosity and improvement.*

Discuss the Impact of Social Support on Personal Growth

"In the vast landscape of personal growth, social support is the fertile soil in which your mindset takes root and blossoms. Let's uncover the profound impact of supportive relationships on your journey toward unlocking your full potential."

The Pillars of Support

- Supportive relationships provide a foundation for personal growth.
- Encouragement and understanding from others fuel confidence and resilience.
- *Example: Visualize the impact of friends cheering you on during challenging times, bolstering your confidence.*

Shared Goals and Encouragement

- Aligned goals within a supportive network enhance motivation and accountability.
- Encouragement from others reinforces the belief that growth is achievable.
- *Example: Imagine pursuing a fitness goal with a workout buddy, sharing encouragement and celebrating milestones together.*

Navigating Challenges Together

- Social support offers a safety net during setbacks and challenges.
- Facing difficulties with others fosters a collective mindset of overcoming obstacles.
- *Example: Consider the reassurance derived from friends during a career setback, providing perspective and motivation.*

Introduce the Concept of Toxic Relationships

"Not all relationships nourish the soil of personal growth; some can poison it. Let's navigate the delicate terrain of toxic relationships—a crucial aspect to understand on your quest for mindset mastery and unlocking your full potential."

Identifying Toxic Traits

● Toxic relationships exhibit harmful traits such as manipulation, constant criticism, or lack of empathy.

● Recognizing these traits is the first step to safeguarding your mindset.

● *Example: Picture a friend who consistently undermines your achievements, eroding your confidence.*

The Erosion of Positive Mindset

● Toxic relationships gradually erode positive mindsets.

● Constant negativity and toxicity can shape a mindset rooted in self-doubt and pessimism.

● *Example: Imagine the impact of a partner who dismisses your aspirations, leading to a diminished belief in your abilities.*

Setting Boundaries for Preservation

● Establishing boundaries is crucial for protecting your mindset.

● Recognizing the impact of toxicity and setting limits is an act of self-preservation.

● *Example: Envision the empowerment derived from distancing yourself from a toxic relationship, creating space for personal growth.*

Closing Thoughts

In the intricate dance between relationships and mindset, each step shapes your journey toward unlocking your full potential. The reciprocity of influence between the two is profound, making it essential to nurture positive connections and guard against toxic influences. As you traverse the landscape of relationships, may your awareness deepen, guiding you toward a supportive network that fosters growth and resilience on your path to mindset mastery.

Remember, the relationships you cultivate are not just companions on your journey but architects of the mindset that will define your destination.

Cultivating Positive Connections

"In the garden of life, positive connections are the vibrant blossoms that enhance the beauty of our journey. Let's explore the art of cultivating positive connections—essential companions on the path to mindset mastery and unlocking your full potential."

Provide Actionable Steps for Building Positive Relationships

Authenticity: Planting the Seeds of Genuine Connection

- Be authentic and true to yourself in interactions.
- Genuine connections flourish when rooted in authenticity.
- *Example: Imagine a friendship where you can be your true self, fostering a connection based on mutual understanding.*

Active Listening: Nurturing Connection Through Understanding

- Practice active listening to truly understand others.
- Listening fosters empathy and strengthens the foundation of a positive connection.
- *Example: Envision a conversation where you feel heard and understood, deepening the bond with the other person.*

Shared Values: Building Bridges of Common Ground

- Identify and embrace shared values with others.
- Common ground forms a solid foundation for lasting positive connections.
- *Example: Picture connecting with someone who shares your passion for a particular cause, creating a bond rooted in shared values.*

Reciprocity: Watering the Growth of Relationships

- Foster reciprocity by giving and receiving support.
- A balanced exchange of care and support sustains positive connections.
- *Example: Visualize a friendship where both parties contribute to each other's well-being, creating a flourishing relationship.*

Discuss the Importance of Empathy in Connections

"In the symphony of connections, empathy is the harmonious melody that binds hearts and minds. Let's unravel the significance of empathy—a key ingredient in the alchemy of positive relationships on your journey to mindset mastery."

Understanding Others' Perspectives: The Compassionate Bridge

- Empathy involves understanding and appreciating others' perspectives.
- Seeing the world through their eyes fosters compassion and deepens connections.
- *Example: Picture a moment when someone empathetically acknowledges your feelings, creating a profound sense of connection.*

Validation: Affirming the Emotions of Others

- Validating others' emotions communicates understanding and support.
- Acknowledging their feelings strengthens the fabric of positive connections.
- *Example: Imagine sharing your challenges with someone who validates your emotions, reinforcing the bond of trust and understanding.*

Compassionate Communication: The Language of Connection

- Communicate with compassion and kindness.
- Empathetic communication builds bridges and nurtures positive relationships.
- *Example: Envision a conversation where empathy guides the words spoken, creating an atmosphere of trust and mutual understanding.*

Explore the Role of Effective Communication in Fostering Positive Relationships

"Communication is the thread that weaves the tapestry of connections. Let's unravel the art of effective communication—an essential skill in cultivating positive relationships that propel you toward mindset mastery and unlocking your full potential."

Clarity: The Foundation of Effective Expression

● **Clearly express thoughts and feelings to avoid misunderstandings.**

● **Clarity promotes understanding and strengthens the fabric of positive connections.**

● *Example: Picture a scenario where clear communication resolves a potential conflict, reinforcing the connection with others.*

Empathetic Expression: Bridging Understanding Through Words

● **Use words that convey empathy and understanding.**

● **Empathetic expression fosters an atmosphere of openness and trust.**

● *Example: Imagine expressing your thoughts in a way that considers others' feelings, creating a space for open and positive communication.*

Feedback and Improvement: Nurturing Growth in Connections

● **Provide constructive feedback to promote growth in relationships.**

● **Feedback, delivered with empathy, contributes to the continuous improvement of connections.**

● *Example: Visualize a feedback exchange between friends that strengthens their bond, fostering mutual growth and understanding.*

Closing Thoughts

Cultivating positive connections is an art that transforms the landscape of your journey toward mindset mastery. By planting seeds of authenticity, practicing active listening, and nurturing empathy, you enrich the soil in which positive relationships flourish. As you communicate with clarity, empathy, and a commitment to growth, may the garden of your connections blossom with vibrant colors, propelling you toward unlocking your full potential. Remember, positive connections are not just companions on your journey—they are the co-authors of the story you're creating, enhancing every chapter with warmth, understanding, and shared growth.

Setting Healthy Boundaries

"In the dance of life, boundaries are the choreography that ensures you move in harmony with your values and well-being. Let's explore the art of setting healthy boundaries—a key to unlocking your full potential and achieving mindset mastery."

Discuss the Importance of Boundaries in Relationships

The Dance of Connection: The Importance of Healthy Boundaries
- Healthy boundaries are the foundation of thriving relationships.
- Boundaries foster respect, communication, and emotional well-being.
- *Example: Imagine a relationship where clear boundaries create a space for mutual growth and understanding.*

Preserving Individuality: The Power of Personal Space
- Boundaries allow individuals to maintain their sense of self.
- Respecting personal space enhances the quality of relationships.
- *Example: Visualize a scenario where respecting personal boundaries strengthens the bond between individuals, allowing each person to flourish.*

Preventing Burnout: Boundaries as Self-Care
- Establishing boundaries prevents burnout and promotes self-care.
- Recognizing limits ensures a sustainable balance in personal and professional life.
- *Example: Picture a work environment where setting boundaries prevents overwhelming stress, fostering a healthier and more productive mindset.*

Provide Guidance on Setting and Communicating Boundaries

"In the grand symphony of life, effective communication is the conductor that ensures your boundaries are heard and respected. Let's unravel the melody of setting and communicating boundaries—an essential skill on your journey to mindset mastery and unlocking your full potential."

Self-Reflection: Understanding Your Needs and Limits

● Reflect on your needs, values, and emotional limits.

● Self-awareness is the first step toward setting meaningful boundaries.

● *Example: Imagine a moment of self-reflection where you identify your priorities, guiding you to set boundaries that align with your values.*

Clear Communication: Expressing Boundaries Effectively

● Clearly communicate your boundaries to others.

● Use assertive and respectful language to convey your needs.

● *Example: Envision a conversation where you express your boundaries with clarity, creating an atmosphere of mutual understanding.*

Consistency: Nurturing Trust Through Boundary Adherence

● Be consistent in upholding your boundaries.

● Consistency builds trust and reinforces the importance of your limits.

● *Example: Picture a scenario where consistency in boundary-setting enhances trust in personal and professional relationships, leading to a positive mindset.*

Explore the Impact of Boundary-Setting on Mindset

"In the canvas of the mind, boundaries are the brushstrokes that define the masterpiece of your mindset. Let's explore the profound impact of setting boundaries—an art that shapes your thoughts, emotions, and overall mindset on the canvas of your life."

Emotional Well-Being: Boundary Setting as a Mental Health Tool

- Boundaries contribute to emotional well-being and mental health.
- Protecting yourself from negativity enhances a positive mindset.
- *Example: Imagine a mindset fortified by healthy emotional boundaries, shielding you from unnecessary stress and fostering mental resilience.*

Empowerment: Boundary-Setting as a Source of Strength

- Setting and maintaining boundaries empower individuals.
- The act of defining limits is an assertion of personal strength and agency.
- *Example: Visualize the empowerment that comes from setting boundaries, cultivating a mindset grounded in self-assurance and resilience.*

Mindset Mastery: The Symbiotic Relationship with Boundaries

- Mastering your mindset involves aligning thoughts with positive boundaries.
- Boundaries create a framework for a growth-oriented and resilient mindset.
- *Example: Picture a mindset that flourishes within the boundaries you've set, embracing challenges as opportunities for growth.*

Closing Thoughts

Setting healthy boundaries is a transformative art—an art that influences the rhythm of your relationships, orchestrates effective communication, and paints the canvas of your mindset. As you dance through life, may the boundaries you set be the graceful steps that guide you toward mindset mastery and the full realization of your potential. Remember, boundaries are not barriers—they are the liberating force that allows you to express yourself authentically, protect your well-being, and nurture a mindset that propels you toward the life you envision. Embrace the dance of boundary-setting, and let it be a melody that resonates with the harmony of your journey.

Navigating Conflict with a Growth Mindset

"In the tapestry of relationships, conflict is the thread that, when woven with a growth mindset, can create a stronger, more resilient bond. Let's embark on the journey of navigating conflict—a pivotal skill on your path to mindset mastery and unlocking your full potential."

Discuss Common Sources of Conflict in Relationships

Miscommunication: The Quagmire of Unspoken Words

- Miscommunication often stems from assumptions and unexpressed expectations.
- Lack of clarity can lead to conflicts that could have been avoided with open communication.
- *Example: Imagine the impact of a simple, honest conversation on preventing misunderstandings that often escalate into conflicts.*

Unmet Expectations: The Breeding Ground for Disappointment

- Unmet expectations can lead to disappointment and frustration.
- Identifying and managing expectations is crucial for maintaining harmony.
- *Example: Visualize a scenario where setting realistic expectations helps prevent conflicts by fostering understanding between individuals.*

Differences in Values: Navigating Diverse Perspectives

- Conflicts arise when values and priorities differ.
- Understanding and respecting diverse perspectives contribute to conflict resolution.
- *Example: Envision a situation where acknowledging and appreciating different values becomes the catalyst for resolving conflicts and strengthening relationships.*

Explore Conflict Resolution Strategies

"In the landscape of relationships, conflict resolution is the compass that guides you through storms, ensuring you emerge stronger on the other side. Let's delve into strategies that not only mend wounds but also cultivate a growth mindset, enriching your journey toward mindset mastery."

Active Listening: The Bridge to Understanding

- Active listening fosters understanding and empathy.
- Hearing and acknowledging the other person's perspective is crucial for resolution.
- *Example: Picture a conversation where active listening transforms conflict into an opportunity for mutual understanding, laying the foundation for resolution.*

Empathy: The Healing Balm in Conflict Resolution

- Empathy allows individuals to connect emotionally, fostering a compassionate environment.
- Putting yourself in the other person's shoes promotes reconciliation.
- *Example: Imagine the transformative power of empathy, turning conflicts into opportunities for connection and shared growth.*

Collaborative Problem-Solving: A Joint Expedition

- Approach conflicts as shared problems to be solved collaboratively.
- Encourage open dialogue to find solutions that benefit all parties involved.
- *Example: Visualize a conflict resolution process where individuals work together, viewing challenges as opportunities to strengthen their connection.*

Introduce the Concept of Using Challenges to Strengthen Relationships

"In the garden of relationships, challenges are the nutrients that, when embraced with a growth mindset, cultivate flourishing bonds. Let's explore how navigating challenges can not only resolve conflicts but also become the fertilizer for a vibrant, thriving connection."

Growth Mindset: Transforming Challenges into Opportunities

● Embrace a growth mindset that views challenges as opportunities for learning and improvement.

● Shift the focus from blame to understanding and growth.

● *Example: Picture a mindset that sees conflicts not as roadblocks but as stepping stones, propelling individuals toward personal and relational growth.*

Learning from Conflict: The Alchemy of Relationship Enhancement

● Extract lessons from conflicts to strengthen the foundation of the relationship.

● View challenges as sources of valuable insights and opportunities for improvement.

● *Example: Imagine a relationship where conflicts serve as catalysts for personal and mutual growth, fostering resilience and adaptability.*

Forgiveness: The Reset Button for Relationship Renewal

● Forgiveness is a powerful tool for moving beyond conflicts.

● Release resentment and use forgiveness as a reset button for a fresh start.

● *Example: Visualize the liberating power of forgiveness, allowing individuals to move forward with a renewed sense of connection and understanding.*

Closing Thoughts

Navigating conflict with a growth mindset is not about avoiding challenges but about turning them into stepping stones for personal and relational development. As you embark on the journey of resolving conflicts, remember that the true measure of success is not the absence of disagreements but the ability to navigate them with empathy, collaboration, and a commitment to continuous growth. Conflict, when approached with a growth mindset, becomes an opportunity for transformation, strengthening the fabric of your relationships and contributing to your mindset mastery. Embrace the challenges, learn from them, and let them become the dynamic forces that propel you toward the full realization of your potential.

Fostering a Supportive Network for Mindset Mastery

"In the dance of personal growth, a supportive network is the partner that makes every step toward mindset mastery more graceful and fulfilling. Let's explore the profound impact of cultivating a tribe that uplifts and propels you toward the realization of your full potential."

Emphasize the Role of a Supportive Network in Mindset Transformation

The Power of Collective Inspiration

- A supportive network acts as a reservoir of inspiration and motivation.
- Surrounding yourself with individuals on similar journeys fosters a collective mindset transformation.
- *Example: Envision the collective energy of a supportive network, each member contributing to a positive and transformative atmosphere.*

Shared Wisdom and Learning

- A network provides diverse perspectives and shared wisdom.
- Learning from others' experiences accelerates your own mindset evolution.
- *Example: Picture a supportive community where the exchange of insights becomes a dynamic force for individual and collective growth.*

Accountability: The Pillar of Progress

- A network holds you accountable for your mindset goals.
- Mutual support ensures that each member stays committed to their personal growth journey.
- *Example: Imagine the impact of a supportive circle, gently nudging you toward your goals and celebrating your victories.*

Discuss the Impact of Peer Influence on Mindset

"In the symphony of mindset transformation, the melodies of peer influence can either harmonize with your growth or introduce discordant notes. Let's

explore the profound impact of those around you on the composition of your mindset."

Positive Peer Influence

- Positive peers inspire and uplift, serving as beacons of growth.
- Shared successes create an environment of celebration and encouragement.
- *Example: Visualize a positive peer influencing your mindset, their success acting as a catalyst for your own aspirations.*

Awareness of Negative Influences

- Negative influences can hinder mindset mastery by introducing doubt and limiting beliefs.
- Recognizing and mitigating the impact of negative influences is essential for growth.
- *Example: Picture a scenario where awareness of negative influences empowers you to protect your mindset from detrimental effects.*

Cultivating a Collective Growth Mindset

- A group with a collective growth mindset reinforces a culture of continuous improvement.
- Celebrating each other's successes contributes to a shared sense of accomplishment.
- *Example: Envision a community where a collective growth mindset becomes the norm, propelling everyone toward their full potential.*

Provide Guidance on Cultivating a Positive Social Environment

"In the garden of your social landscape, cultivating a positive environment is the fertile ground where the seeds of mindset mastery blossom into vibrant, resilient blooms. Let's explore practical guidance on sowing the seeds of positivity in your social circles."

Intentional Relationship Building

- Actively seek and nurture relationships that align with your growth goals.
- Prioritize connections that contribute positively to your mindset journey.

- *Example: Imagine the impact of intentionally building relationships that support and enhance your mindset aspirations.*

Open Communication and Vulnerability

- Foster an environment where open communication and vulnerability are valued.

- Honest conversations create deeper connections and foster mutual support.

- *Example: Picture a social circle where open communication allows for shared struggles and triumphs, creating an authentic bond.*

Setting Healthy Boundaries

- Establish clear boundaries to protect your mindset and well-being.

- Communicate your needs and ensure that relationships respect these boundaries.

- *Example: Visualize the positive impact of setting healthy boundaries, creating a space that nurtures your mindset growth.*

Closing Thoughts

A supportive network is not just a backdrop in the theatre of your mindset transformation; it's a co-star that shapes the narrative and propels you toward your full potential. As you curate your social environment, remember that every relationship, positive or negative, plays a part in your mindset symphony. Embrace those who uplift and inspire, be mindful of influences that hinder your growth, and actively cultivate a positive social landscape. Your mindset mastery is a collaborative effort, and the strength of your network is the wind beneath your wings, carrying you to heights you might not achieve alone. Cherish the relationships that contribute to your growth, and let them be the guiding stars on your journey to unleashing your full potential.

Chapter 10
Sustainable Mindset Mastery

Reflecting on the Journey

"In the grand tapestry of mindset mastery, reflection is the mirror that reveals the intricate threads woven throughout your transformative journey. Let's embark on a thoughtful exploration of the power of self-reflection and how it serves as a compass guiding you toward your full potential."

Encourage Readers to Reflect on Their Mindset Transformation

The Mirror of Self-Reflection

- Self-reflection is the compass that guides you on your mindset transformation.

- Encouraging readers to pause and introspect about their mindset evolution.

- *Example: Think of self-reflection as a mirror reflecting not just your current state but the transformative journey you've been on.*

Acknowledging the Journey

- Reflecting on the milestones achieved in mindset mastery.

- Recognizing the growth, shifts, and new perspectives gained.

- *Example: Imagine taking a moment to acknowledge the distance traveled, appreciating the steps taken on the path to mindset mastery.*

Learning from Challenges

- Challenges are stepping stones; reflecting on them is crucial for growth.

- Encouraging readers to view setbacks as opportunities for learning.

- *Example: Picture challenges as teachers, imparting valuable lessons on your journey to mindset mastery.*

Provide Prompts for Self-Assessment

"In the quiet space of self-assessment, you discover the contours of your mindset landscape—what elevates you, what holds you back. Let's delve into prompts that invite introspection, helping you map the terrain of your evolving mindset."

Questioning Limiting Beliefs

● Encouraging readers to identify and challenge limiting beliefs.

● Prompts like "What beliefs have restricted my potential?" stimulate self-awareness.

● *Example: Reflect on the beliefs that might be silently sabotaging your progress, and ask yourself why you hold onto them.*

Gratitude as a Reflective Lens

● Using gratitude as a lens to reflect on positive transformations.

● Prompts such as "What am I grateful for in my mindset journey?" foster a positive mindset.

● *Example: Imagine viewing your journey through the lens of gratitude, highlighting the positive changes and growth.*

Exploring Shifts in Perspective

● Inviting readers to examine shifts in mindset perspectives.

● Prompts like "How has my perception of challenges changed?" encourage introspection.

● *Example: Picture the various angles from which you've approached challenges, realizing the evolving nature of your mindset.*

Celebrate the Progress Made in the Mindset Mastery Journey

"Amidst the hustle for progress, pausing to celebrate is the fuel that sustains your journey. Let's revel in the joyous celebration of the progress made, no matter how small, in the wondrous odyssey of mindset mastery."

The Joy of Small Wins

- Emphasizing the significance of celebrating small victories.
- The cumulative effect of acknowledging progress.
- *Example: Imagine the joy of a puzzle coming together, piece by piece, celebrating each small win on your mindset journey.*

Mindset Evolution as a Dynamic Process

- Highlighting that mindset mastery is an ongoing, dynamic process.
- Celebrating the journey itself, not just the destination.
- *Example: Envision mindset mastery as a dynamic dance, celebrating each step, spin, and twirl as part of the joyous rhythm of growth.*

Creating Milestone Rituals

- Introducing the idea of creating personal milestone rituals.
- These rituals mark significant points in the mindset transformation.
- *Example: Picture creating a simple ritual, like writing a letter to yourself, to commemorate and celebrate your mindset milestones.*

Closing Thoughts

As you stand at the crossroads of reflection, self-assessment, and celebration, remember that this is not the culmination but a checkpoint in your ongoing journey of mindset mastery. The mirror of self-reflection reflects not just who you are but the potential for who you can become. Embrace the prompts that invite you to explore your mindset landscape, celebrate the progress made, and continue this transformative journey with the knowledge that each step forward is a victory worth savoring. In the dance of mindset mastery, reflection is the rhythm that keeps you attuned to the melody of your own growth.

Creating a Personalized Mindset Maintenance Plan

"Just as a well-tended garden thrives, so does your mindset. Let's delve into the art of creating a personalized mindset maintenance plan that not only sustains but nourishes your growth, ensuring the bloom of your full potential."

Guide Readers in Developing a Sustainable Mindset Maintenance Plan

Understanding Your Mindset Ecosystem

- Introduce the idea that the mindset is like an ecosystem.
- Encourage readers to identify elements that contribute positively and negatively.
- *Example: Imagine your mindset as a garden; some thoughts and habits are flowers, while others may be weeds. What do you want to nurture, and what needs pruning?*

Identifying Key Maintenance Practices

- Discuss fundamental practices for a healthy mindset.
- Emphasize the importance of self-care, positive affirmations, and gratitude.
- *Example: Consider self-care as watering your mindset garden. Without it, even the most resilient plants can wither.*

Tailoring Practices to Personal Preferences

- Guide readers to customize practices based on personal preferences.
- Ensure that the maintenance plan aligns with individual lifestyles.
- *Example: If meditation feels like weeding to you, find alternative practices like walking or journaling that still contribute to a thriving mindset.*

Discuss the Role of Ongoing Learning and Growth

"Just as a river shapes the land it flows through, continuous learning shapes your mindset. Let's navigate the currents of ongoing learning and growth, understanding how they sculpt the landscape of your unlimited potential."

Embracing a Growth Mindset

● **Explain the concept of a growth mindset.**

● **Emphasize that challenges are opportunities for learning and growth.**

● *Example: Imagine your mindset as a riverbank; a fixed mindset is rigid like concrete, while a growth mindset is fluid, shaping the terrain.*

Curating a Learning Toolbox

● **Encourage readers to build a toolbox for continuous learning.**

● **Include books, podcasts, courses, and experiences.**

● *Example: Picture your learning toolbox as a treasure chest. Open it regularly to discover the gems that contribute to your mindset mastery.*

Learning from Diverse Sources

● **Highlight the importance of diverse perspectives in learning.**

● **Encourage exploring different genres, cultures, and viewpoints.**

● *Example: Just as a garden thrives with diverse flora, your mindset flourishes when fed with a variety of ideas and experiences.*

Provide Tools for Adapting the Plan to Evolving Life Circumstances

"Life is a dynamic journey, and so is your mindset maintenance plan. Let's equip you with tools to adjust, adapt, and ensure your plan not only survives but thrives amidst the ever-changing seasons of life."

Regular Check-ins and Adjustments

- Advocate for regular evaluations of the mindset maintenance plan.
- Encourage readers to adjust practices based on effectiveness.
- *Example: Imagine your mindset maintenance plan as a GPS. Periodic check-ins ensure you're on the right route to unleashing your potential.*

Flexibility in Adversity

- Discuss the importance of flexibility during challenging times.
- Provide tools to modify the plan to accommodate stress or adversity.
- *Example: A resilient mindset is like bamboo, bending but not breaking in the storm. Adapt your maintenance plan to weather life's challenges.*

Community and Accountability

- Emphasize the role of a supportive community.
- Encourage readers to share their maintenance plans for mutual support.
- *Example: A garden flourishes when tended by a community. Similarly, your mindset thrives when nurtured collectively.*

Closing Thoughts

Your personalized mindset maintenance plan is not a rigid set of rules but a dynamic blueprint for growth. Cultivate practices that resonate with you, embrace continuous learning, and equip yourself with the tools to adapt to life's twists and turns. Just as a well-cared-for garden yields a bountiful harvest, your mindset, when tended with care, will unleash the full spectrum of your potential. It's a journey, not a destination, and your mindset maintenance plan is the compass guiding you toward the boundless horizons of your own growth.

Mindset Mastery Beyond the Individual

"The ripple effect of mindset mastery goes beyond personal growth, transforming communities and organizations. Let's explore the profound impact of a mastered mindset on a collective scale, opening doors to a world where everyone can unleash their full potential."

Explore the Broader Impact of Mindset Mastery on Communities and Organizations

From Individuals to Collectives

- Discuss the interconnectedness of individuals within communities and organizations.
- Highlight that mindset mastery isn't just about personal success but contributes to the collective well-being.
- *Example: Imagine a garden where every flower contributes to the beauty of the whole. Similarly, individual mindset mastery enhances the collective bloom.*

Creating Positive Work Environments

- Explore how mindset mastery fosters healthier workplace cultures.
- Discuss the role of positive mindset in teamwork, communication, and productivity.
- *Example: A workplace with a growth-oriented mindset is like a thriving ecosystem. Every member contributes to the overall health and productivity.*

Empowering Leadership

- Emphasize the impact of leaders' mindset on an entire organization.
- Discuss how leaders can inspire a positive mindset culture.
- *Example: A leader's mindset is like the sun in a garden, providing the necessary energy for every aspect of the organization to flourish.*

Discuss the Role of Mindset in Societal Progress

"Societal progress begins with individual transformations. Let's unravel the threads connecting mindset to the tapestry of societal advancement, where collective growth becomes a catalyst for positive change."

Mindset as the Foundation for Change

● Discuss how societal progress hinges on the mindset of its members.

● Emphasize the importance of a collective shift towards growth-oriented thinking.

● *Example: Picture societal progress as a house. A solid foundation of positive mindset ensures its longevity and resilience.*

Innovation and Problem-Solving

● Explore the role of mindset in fostering innovation and addressing societal challenges.

● Discuss historical examples of societies that embraced a progressive mindset.

● *Example: Think of societal progress as a puzzle. A growth mindset helps communities solve complex problems, creating a picture of a better future.*

Mindset's Impact on Social Dynamics

● Examine how mindset influences social interactions and relationships.

● Discuss the importance of empathy, collaboration, and understanding in societal harmony.

● *Example: A society with a growth mindset is like a garden where different flowers coexist, each contributing to the vibrant beauty of the whole.*

Encourage Readers to Share and Spread the Mindset Mastery Journey

"Just as a single seed can grow into a forest, the journey of mindset mastery can flourish when shared. Let's delve into the power of spreading the wisdom, inspiring a collective wave of growth and transformation."

The Butterfly Effect of Personal Growth

- Illustrate how one person's mindset transformation can inspire others.
- Share stories of individuals whose journey has sparked positive change in their communities.
- *Example: Think of personal growth as a butterfly's flutter. The effects may be subtle, but they can create a storm of positive change.*

Creating a Chain Reaction

- Encourage readers to share their mindset mastery experiences with friends, family, and colleagues.
- Discuss the potential of a ripple effect, where small changes accumulate into a wave of collective growth.
- *Example: Imagine mindset mastery as a shared candle. Lighting another's candle doesn't diminish yours; it multiplies the light.*

Utilizing Social Platforms for Good

- Discuss the role of social media in spreading positive messages.
- Encourage readers to contribute to the online space with uplifting content.
- *Example: Social media is like a global garden. Plant seeds of positivity and watch them bloom across continents.*

Closing Thoughts

Mindset mastery extends far beyond the individual—it weaves through the fabric of communities, organizations, and societies. As you embark on this journey, remember that your growth contributes to a collective transformation. Share your experiences, be the catalyst for positive change, and together, let's create a world where everyone can unleash their full potential.

Staying Connected to Growth

"The journey of mindset mastery is like tending to a garden. To ensure continuous blossoming, staying connected to growth is essential. Let's explore strategies to cultivate a mindset that flourishes over time."

Provide Strategies for Staying Connected to Personal Growth

Cultivating a Growth Routine

- Establish the importance of daily habits that contribute to personal development.
- Discuss simple routines, such as morning reflections or evening gratitude practices, that foster growth.
- *Example: Like watering your garden each day, a growth routine ensures your mindset is nurtured consistently, leading to a thriving mental landscape.*

Embracing a Learning Mindset

- Highlight the role of curiosity and a willingness to learn in sustaining personal growth.
- Discuss the benefits of exploring new topics, reading diverse materials, and engaging in continuous education.
- *Example: Just as a garden thrives when new seeds are planted, your mind flourishes when you embrace the joy of learning.*

Setting Progressive Goals

- Encourage readers to establish achievable yet challenging goals for ongoing growth.
- Discuss the satisfaction of achieving milestones and how it fuels further motivation.
- *Example: Similar to tending to different plants in your garden, setting and achieving goals diversifies your personal growth, creating a vibrant mindset.*

Discuss the Importance of Regular Mindset Check-ins

"Imagine a garden left unattended—without regular care, it wilts. Similarly, to sustain mindset mastery, regular check-ins are crucial. Let's delve into the significance of assessing and nurturing your mindset consistently."

Reflection as a Growth Tool

● Emphasize the power of reflection in understanding one's mindset.

● Discuss the benefits of introspection, acknowledging achievements, and identifying areas for improvement.

● *Example: Regularly inspecting your mental garden allows you to prune negativity and cultivate positivity.*

Adapting to Changes

● Discuss the inevitability of changes in life and how mindset check-ins help adapt to evolving circumstances.

● Highlight the importance of flexibility and resilience in maintaining a positive mindset.

● *Example: Just as a garden adjusts to different seasons, your mindset should adapt to life's changes, thriving in every circumstance.*

Identifying Limiting Beliefs

● Explore the concept of limiting beliefs and their impact on personal growth.

● Provide guidance on recognizing and challenging these beliefs during mindset check-ins.

● *Example: Weeding out limiting beliefs is like removing obstacles from your mental garden, allowing your mindset to flourish.*

Explore the Concept of Mentorship in Sustaining Mindset Mastery

"In the garden of personal development, a mentor is like an experienced gardener—offering guidance, support, and insights. Let's explore how mentorship can be the sunlight that nourishes your mindset, helping it reach new heights."

Benefits of Mentorship

● Discuss the transformative impact of having a mentor on mindset mastery.

● Explore how a mentor provides guidance, encouragement, and a fresh perspective.

● *Example: A mentor is like a seasoned gardener sharing their wisdom, helping your mindset bloom in ways you hadn't imagined.*

Finding the Right Mentor

● Guide readers on selecting mentors aligned with their growth goals.

● Discuss the importance of diverse perspectives and mentorship from various areas of life.

● *Example: Just as different plants thrive in specific conditions, finding the right mentor ensures tailored guidance for your unique mindset needs.*

Building a Supportive Community

● Emphasize the role of a supportive network in sustaining mindset mastery.

● Discuss the collective strength of a community where individuals uplift each other.

● *Example: A garden flourishes when various plants support each other. Similarly, a community of like-minded individuals nurtures a collective mindset of growth.*

Closing Thoughts

Staying connected to growth is not a one-time task but a continuous journey. Through intentional routines, regular check-ins, and the support of mentors and communities, your mindset can evolve and flourish. Like a well-tended garden, your mindset has the potential to be a source of joy, inspiration, and continuous growth. Cultivate it with care, and watch as it unfolds into its fullest potential.

Empowering Others to Master Their Mindset

"Just as a candle doesn't lose its flame by lighting another, empowering others in mindset mastery creates a brighter world. Let's explore the profound impact of guiding others on their journey to unlocking their full potential."

Share Stories of Individuals Who Inspired Others Through Mindset Mastery

The Mentor's Tale

- *Example: Meet Sarah, a mentor who transformed her life through mindset mastery. By sharing her experiences, struggles, and triumphs, she inspired countless others to embark on their own journeys of self-discovery.*

From Doubt to Belief

- *Example: John, once crippled by self-doubt, discovered the power of positive thinking. His story resonated with friends and family, igniting a wave of mindset transformation that rippled through his entire community.*

Small Changes, Big Impact

- *Example: Emily's simple mindset shifts not only brought her personal success but also influenced her colleagues. Soon, the workplace became a hub of motivation and collaboration, showcasing the transformative power of mindset mastery.*

Discuss the Ripple Effect of a Positive Mindset on Those Around Us

"Ever skipped a stone across a pond and watched the ripples spread? Similarly, a positive mindset creates waves of change. Let's dive into the fascinating ripple effect, exploring how our mindset influences those we encounter."

Radiating Positivity

● Discuss how an individual's positive mindset can uplift the spirits of those around them.

● *Example: Mark's infectious positivity in the office not only improved his work but also created an environment where colleagues felt motivated and engaged.*

Inspiring Growth in Others

● Explore how personal growth resulting from mindset mastery becomes a source of inspiration for others.

● *Example: Tina's commitment to learning and self-improvement inspired her friends to pursue their goals, creating a community driven by a collective growth mindset.*

Cultivating a Supportive Network

● Emphasize how a positive mindset fosters the creation of a supportive community.

● *Example: The friendship between James and Emma, rooted in mutual encouragement and positive reinforcement, illustrates the power of a supportive network.*

Encourage Readers to Become Ambassadors of Mindset Mastery

"Imagine a world where everyone is an ambassador of mindset mastery—spreading positivity, inspiring change, and unlocking potential. It starts with you. Let's explore how you can become a beacon of mindset empowerment."

Lead by Example

• Discuss the impact of personal growth on influencing those around you.

• *Example: Becoming an ambassador means embodying the principles of mindset mastery. By consistently showcasing a positive mindset, you inspire others to follow suit.*

Share Personal Experiences

• Encourage readers to open up about their own mindset journey, creating a culture of vulnerability and growth.

• *Example: Your story, with all its highs and lows, can resonate with someone facing similar challenges. Sharing your experiences fosters connection and encourages others to embrace mindset mastery.*

Create a Culture of Growth

• Discuss how fostering a culture of continuous learning and improvement can positively impact communities.

• *Example: Initiating book clubs, discussion forums, or workshops on mindset mastery within your community helps create an environment that supports and nurtures personal development.*

Closing Thoughts

Empowering others in mindset mastery is not just a gift to them; it's a gift to the world. By sharing stories, understanding the ripple effect, and becoming ambassadors of positive change, individuals can collectively create a community that thrives on the principles of growth and empowerment. As you embark on this journey, remember: your influence is more powerful than you think, and the seeds you plant today can blossom into a forest of empowered minds tomorrow.

Mindset Mastery: Unleashing Your Full Potential

Summary of Key Takeaways

"Embarking on the journey of mindset mastery is like opening a treasure chest of personal growth. Let's dive into the key takeaways from this transformative exploration, unlocking the secrets to unleashing your full potential."

The Power of Mindset

- Emphasize the impact of beliefs on personal growth.
- Explore the neuroscience behind mindset development.
- Provide actionable steps for cultivating a growth mindset.

The Role of Self-Awareness

- Discuss the connection between self-awareness and mindset.
- Introduce mindfulness practices for enhancing self-awareness.
- Highlight the importance of recognizing and transforming negative thought patterns.

Goal Setting and Visualization

- Explore the power of clear goals on mindset.
- Introduce visualization techniques for success.
- Discuss affirmations as tools for goal achievement.

Embracing Change and Adaptability

- Discuss the inevitability of change and its impact on mindset.
- Provide tools for cultivating an adaptive mindset.
- Explore the transformative power of leveraging change for personal growth.

Building Resilience

- Define resilience and its role in mindset mastery.
- Discuss emotional and cognitive resilience techniques.
- Share stories of individuals demonstrating resilience in major life changes.

Cultivating Positive Habits

- Explore the habit loop and its impact on mindset.
- Provide strategies for identifying and breaking negative habits.

- Emphasize the importance of sustaining positive habits for long-term success.

Gratitude and Positive Affirmations

- Explore the psychological benefits of gratitude.
- Discuss the role of affirmations in mindset transformation.
- Share techniques for overcoming negativity bias with positivity.

Mindful Decision Making

- Discuss the cognitive processes involved in decision-making.
- Introduce mindfulness techniques for effective decision-making.
- Explore aligning decisions with values and goals.

Nurturing Positive Relationships

- Explore the reciprocal influence of relationships and mindset.
- Discuss the impact of social support and the importance of empathy.
- Provide guidance on setting healthy boundaries and navigating conflict with a growth mindset.

Sustainable Mindset Mastery

- Encourage reflection on the mindset transformation journey.
- Guide readers in developing a personalized mindset maintenance plan.
- Explore the broader impact of mindset mastery and staying connected to personal growth.

Recap the Essential Concepts Explored in Each Chapter

"Let's take a stroll down memory lane, revisiting the landscapes of each chapter. Together, we'll recap the essential concepts, solidifying the foundation of mindset mastery you've built throughout this journey."

Chapter 1: The Power of Mindset

- Embracing challenges for a growth mindset.
- Identifying and challenging limiting beliefs.
- Applying growth mindset to personal goals.

Chapter 2: The Role of Self-Awareness

- Mindfulness practices for enhancing self-awareness.
- Recognizing and transforming negative thought patterns.
- Implementing self-awareness in decision-making.

Chapter 3: Goal Setting and Visualization

- The impact of clear goals on mindset.
- Visualization techniques for success.
- Affirmations for goal achievement.

Chapter 4: Embracing Change and Adaptability

- Cultivating an adaptive mindset.
- Tools for embracing uncertainty.
- Leveraging change for personal growth.

Chapter 5: Building Resilience

- Emotional and cognitive resilience techniques.
- Cognitive restructuring for resilience.
- Resilience in the face of major life changes.

Chapter 6: Cultivating Positive Habits

- The habit loop and its impact on mindset.
- Strategies for breaking negative habits.
- Sustaining positive habits for long-term success.

Chapter 7: Gratitude and Positive Affirmations

- The psychological benefits of gratitude.
- Creating a positive affirmation practice.

Emphasize the Transformative Power of Mindset Mastery

"Mindset mastery is the magic wand that turns dreams into reality. Let's unravel the enchantment, understanding the profound transformation your mindset can bring to your life."

Personal Growth

- Discuss the journey from a fixed to a growth mindset.
- Share stories of personal transformations.
- Emphasize the continuous improvement mindset.

Resilience and Adversity

- Highlight the role of mindset in bouncing back from setbacks.
- Explore the concept of post-traumatic growth.
- Share examples of individuals who turned adversity into opportunity.

Goal Achievement

- Discuss the impact of mindset on setting and achieving goals.
- Share success stories rooted in the power of mindset.
- Emphasize the importance of celebrating achievements.

Positive Habits and Rituals

- Explore the cumulative impact of sustained positive habits.
- Discuss the role of habits in shaping your future.
- Emphasize the transformative power of positive daily rituals.

Mindful Decision-Making

- Discuss how mindful decision-making shapes your life.
- Explore the connection between clarity and decision-making.
- Emphasize learning from both successful and failed decisions.

Gratitude and Positivity

- Highlight how gratitude turns what you have into enough.
- Discuss the transformative power of positive affirmations.
- Emphasize overcoming negativity bias with positivity.

Nurturing Relationships

- Explore how positive relationships influence mindset.

- Discuss the impact of social support and empathy.
- Emphasize the importance of setting healthy boundaries.

Cultivating Adaptability

- Discuss how embracing change leads to personal development.
- Explore the psychological responses to change.
- Emphasize the role of adaptability in resilience.

Continuous Learning

- Discuss the importance of continuous learning in mindset mastery.
- Explore the impact of ongoing growth on mindset.
- Emphasize the transformative nature of a growth-oriented mindset.

Impact Beyond the Individual

- Explore the broader impact of mindset mastery on communities and organizations.
- Discuss the role of mindset in societal progress.
- Encourage readers to share and spread the mindset mastery journey.

Final Words of Encouragement

"Congratulations on reaching the summit of mindset mastery! As you stand on this peak of personal growth, take a moment to savor the accomplishment. Let's wrap up this journey with words that inspire, uplift, and propel you forward."

"Dear reader, you've ventured into the realms of your mind, unlocked the gates to growth, and embraced the transformative power of mindset mastery. As you stand at the culmination of this journey, remember these words: your potential is boundless, your growth unstoppable, and your mindset, the compass guiding you to new horizons.

"In the vast landscape of your future, you hold the brush to paint the canvas of your dreams. Every stroke is an affirmation of your resilience, adaptability, and unwavering belief in your potential. The mindset you've cultivated is not just a tool; it's a lifelong companion, a beacon illuminating the path to continuous growth.

"Life is a journey of constant evolution, and you're now equipped with the wisdom to navigate its twists and turns. Remember, setbacks are not roadblocks but stepping stones, and each challenge is an opportunity to demonstrate the mastery you've cultivated.

"As you move forward, let your mindset be a source of courage, your companion in the face of change, and your guiding light through the uncharted territories of personal growth. This is not the end but a new beginning—a beginning where you are the author of your story, the architect of your destiny.

"May your mindset be forever resilient, your goals perpetually achievable, and your journey a testament to the boundless potential within you. You are not just unleashing your full potential; you are becoming a masterpiece in the gallery of your own creation.

"With heartfelt congratulations and the utmost belief in your continued success,

Your mindset mastery companion."

Motivate Readers to Continue Their Mindset Mastery Journey

"The journey doesn't end here; it's a perpetual exploration of growth and potential. Let's pave the way for your next steps, keeping the flames of mindset mastery burning bright within you."

Set New Goals

- Encourage readers to set fresh, inspiring goals.
- Discuss the power of continuous goal-setting in mindset mastery.
- Emphasize refining goals based on personal growth.

Embrace Challenges

- Remind readers that challenges are opportunities for growth.
- Discuss the concept of challenges as catalysts for positive change.
- Share stories of individuals who turned challenges into triumphs.

Reflect and Learn

- Encourage regular reflection on the mindset transformation journey.
- Provide prompts for self-assessment and introspection.
- Emphasize the value of learning from experiences, both positive and negative.

Stay Connected to Growth

- Provide strategies for staying connected to personal growth.
- Discuss the importance of regular mindset check-ins.
- Explore the concept of mentorship in sustaining mindset mastery.

Share Your Journey

- Encourage readers to become ambassadors of mindset mastery.
- Discuss the ripple effect of a positive mindset on those around them.
- Share tips for sharing their mindset journey with others.

Provide a Final Inspirational Quote or Anecdote

"Let's conclude this chapter with a touch of inspiration—a quote or anecdote that encapsulates the essence of mindset mastery and serves as a guiding light for the journey ahead."

"As you continue your journey, remember the wisdom encapsulated in the following quote:

" 'The only limit to our realization of tomorrow will be our doubts of today.' — Franklin D. Roosevelt

This powerful reminder echoes the core philosophy of mindset mastery: that the only limits we face are those we place upon ourselves. Doubts and uncertainties are mere clouds passing through the vast sky of your potential. As you venture forward, keep this truth close to your heart, dispelling doubts, embracing uncertainties, and unfurling the wings of your boundless potential.

May this quote be a beacon, illuminating the path to a future where doubts are replaced with confidence, limits with possibilities, and each step forward becomes a testament to the remarkable journey you've undertaken.

With this guiding light, step boldly into the future, for it is a canvas awaiting the brushstrokes of your resilience, adaptability, and unwavering belief in your potential."

Call to Action

"As we draw the curtains on this book, it's not just an ending but a commencement of a lifelong journey. Let's explore the call to action that beckons you to apply, share, and perpetuate the principles of mindset mastery."

Apply the Principles

● Encourage readers to immediately apply the mindset mastery principles.

● Provide practical steps for integrating these principles into daily life.

● Emphasize the transformative impact of consistent application.

Share Your Story

● Urge readers to share their mindset transformation stories.

● Provide platforms or communities for sharing experiences.

● Discuss the potential positive impact on others.

Inspire Others

● Encourage readers to become ambassadors of mindset mastery.

● Discuss the ripple effect of inspiring others through personal growth.

● Share examples of individuals who inspired change in their communities.

Connect with Like-Minded Individuals

● Suggest joining communities or groups focused on personal development.

● Discuss the value of peer support in sustaining mindset mastery.

● Share resources for finding and connecting with like-minded individuals.

Continue Learning

● Emphasize the importance of continuous learning in the journey.

● Recommend books, courses, or resources for ongoing personal development.

● Discuss the role of curiosity and openness to new ideas.

Encourage Readers to Apply the Principles Learned

"Knowledge gains its true power when applied. Let's delve into practical ways for readers to take the principles learned on this mindset mastery journey and apply them to their lives."

Create an Action Plan

• Guide readers in creating a personalized action plan based on the book's principles.

• Break down the plan into manageable steps.

• Emphasize the importance of consistency in implementing the plan.

Daily Reflection

• Encourage daily reflection on mindset and personal growth.

• Provide prompts for self-reflection.

• Discuss the impact of consistent reflection on mindset transformation.

Set Short-Term and Long-Term Goals

• Discuss the power of setting both short-term and long-term goals.

• Guide readers in defining achievable milestones.

• Emphasize the connection between goals and mindset mastery.

Surround Yourself with Positivity

• Discuss the influence of the environment on mindset.

• Encourage creating a positive and growth-oriented social circle.

• Share practical tips for fostering positivity in daily life.

Embrace Challenges

• Remind readers that challenges are opportunities for growth.

• Discuss the mindset needed to approach challenges positively.

• Share stories of individuals who turned challenges into stepping stones.

Provide Resources for Ongoing Support and Learning

"The journey of mindset mastery is ongoing, and resources are the compass guiding you. Let's explore a treasure trove of tools, books, and communities that offer continuous support for your growth."

Recommended Reading

● Provide a list of recommended books for further exploration.

● Summarize each book's key concepts and how they complement mindset mastery.

● Include a variety of genres to cater to different preferences.

Online Courses and Workshops

● Recommend online courses or workshops related to mindset mastery.

● Highlight the benefits of structured learning experiences.

● Include platforms or websites where readers can find relevant courses.

Podcasts and Videos

● Suggest podcasts or YouTube channels that delve into personal development.

● Provide a brief overview of each recommendation.

● Emphasize the accessibility and flexibility of audio and video content.

Communities and Forums

● Recommend online communities or forums focused on mindset mastery.

● Discuss the value of connecting with like-minded individuals.

● Provide guidance on participating in discussions and sharing experiences.

Coaching and Mentorship

● Discuss the benefits of coaching or mentorship in personal development.

● Provide tips on finding a suitable coach or mentor.

● **Emphasize the personalized support and guidance available through such relationships.**

"As you navigate the sea of continuous growth, let these resources be your companions, guiding lights, and sources of inspiration. Remember, the journey of mindset mastery is not a solo expedition but a collective exploration of human potential."